"For anyone wanting to elevate their interview skills, this superb book does the job! Filled with powerful advice along with essential 'how-tos,' Sam Owens's book delivers both wonderful insight and practical application. He generously shares his wisdom (and his mistakes) openly with the reader in an easy-to-follow format as he provides an illuminating path to follow. The perfect graduation gift!"
—STEPHEN M. R. COVEY, *New York Times* and #1 *Wall Street Journal* best-selling author of *The Speed of Trust* and *Trust and Inspire*

"Sam Owen's *I Hate Job Interviews* is a game changer for anyone grappling with the nerve-racking world of job interviewing. Sam delivers brutally honest advice doused with humor, making it an engaging and inspiring read. What sets this book apart is the incorporation of transformative personal experiences, both from the author and job seekers mentored by Sam, to illustrate practical and proven frameworks for excelling in the job interview process. If you're ready to shift from anxiety to confidence and secure the job you want, this book is your indispensable guide."
—MIKE NEUFFER, career director, BYU Marriott School of Business

"The best candidate doesn't get the job, the best interviewer does. Sam Owens breaks down every element you need to think about to improve your interviewing skills so you can land the job. I've been a recruiter for a decade and have seen firsthand how not being prepared for an interview can cost you opportunities. This book will help anyone who is looking to grow their interview skills and land jobs they want."
—JOEL LALGEE, executive recruiter and social media personality

"Preparation breeds confidence. Sam Owens's book will give you the right tools and tricks to prepare for your high-stakes interview, so that you will feel like you are putting your best foot forward."
—SARAH JOHNSTON, executive résumé writer and founder of Briefcase Coach

T0026640

i hate job interviews

stop stressing.
start performing.
get the job you want.

sam owens

HarperCollins
Leadership

An Imprint of HarperCollins

Published by HarperCollins Leadership, an imprint of HarperCollins Focus LLC.

Any internet addresses, phone numbers, or company or product information printed in this book are offered as a resource and are not intended in any way to be or to imply an endorsement by HarperCollins Leadership, nor does HarperCollins Leadership vouch for the existence, content, or services of these sites, phone numbers, companies, or products beyond the life of this book.

ISBN 978-1-4002-4590-1 (eBook)
ISBN 978-1-4002-4589-5 (TP)

Library of Congress Control Number: 2023948688

Printed in the United States of America

24 25 26 27 28 LBC 5 4 3 2 1

contents.

Chapter Six
Tell Compelling Stories:

Chapter Seven
Use Simple Frameworks:

Chapter Eight
Know Thyself:

Chapter Nine
Avoid Land Mines:

Chapter Ten
Strike Last, Strike Hard:

Chapter Eleven
Know Your Worth:

Conclusion:

how to use this book.

This book is meant to be read cover to cover. That's why it's organized sequentially, taking you step-by-step to job interview awesomeness. If you follow each step, you'll be at your best in your next interview.

But this book is also meant to be a quick reference. That's why it's organized into discrete sections, allowing you to easily access a specific skill you'd like to improve.

The way you read this book depends on your situation. Are you planning to switch jobs in the next year and want to make sure you are fully ready? If so, read it from start to finish and work through each step in sequence. Or do you have an interview in two days and are still concerned about that case question you botched last time? If so, cut straight to the chapter on scenario questions and get what you need, fast. You can read the rest after your interview.

My hope is that this book will be a useful reference throughout your career. The core principles of job interviewing haven't changed much in the last thirty years, and they likely won't change much in the next thirty. If you are anything like the average worker, you'll switch jobs several times in your career. This book will be there for you each time.

introduction.

The Hatred Is Real

Heather started to cry fifteen minutes into our coaching session. She had held it together during the initial pleasantries of our call, but once she began talking about her current job situation the tears started flowing. Heather was being pushed out of her current organization after a decade of dedicated service. Now in midcareer, she faced the daunting prospect of putting herself back on the market and interviewing for other jobs.

She apologized for her emotions, but I assured her that no apology was needed. Crying was perfectly normal, even expected, from someone in her current career predicament. Over the years, I'd coached several people like Heather—talented but frustrated professionals suddenly unsure about their futures. Job seeking can be a discouraging experience fraught with anxiety, fear, and loneliness. Some of my clients compare the feelings of job searching to those of getting a divorce. Just the thought of starting over and putting themselves back on the market is unappealing. But compound that with the fact that they've been out of the game for so long and are now in a different phase of life, and it's downright exhausting.

The most daunting part of the whole process is the job interview, the climax of the job search. Job interviewing is a high-stakes, winner-takes-all game. It's where all the energy of the job search culminates into a one-hour conversation. There are no do-overs, no second chances, no edits or redactions. With that kind of pressure, I completely understand why so many people hate job interviews.

I told Heather that things were going to work out and that I could help her land a fantastic job. I had developed a coaching program that includes a set of simple, step-by-step frameworks that are easy to understand and can be applied by anyone—from someone just coming out of college to a seasoned executive needing a refresher course. With these tools, Heather would be able to interview at her absolute, confident best.

Before I get into these tools, you should know that I was once a first-class job interview hater myself. My story starts in 2007 when I entered business school, brimming with confidence about my career prospects. The job market was strong, with unemployment hovering at just under 5 percent; I had a good résumé, having recently worked for a well-known consulting firm in Washington, DC; and the MBA program I had recently enrolled in had a track record of placing graduates with great companies like Microsoft, Procter & Gamble, Walmart, and Amazon. With a little energy and charisma, landing a great internship after my first year was guaranteed.

Or so I thought.

During my first year of school, I interviewed with Target, Walmart, the Union Pacific Railroad, and Nestlé. I didn't receive a single internship offer. It's not that these companies weren't hiring interns; they weren't hiring *me*. Every rejection was a blow to my confidence, and I wondered why I wasn't getting offers. I was clearly qualified on paper because I was being selected to interview.

Plus, I was personable and likable, at least in my humble opinion. Yet it was my classmates, not me, who were getting internship offers—sometimes two or three of them. I thought interviewing was going to be my strongest advantage going into my MBA program, and it turned out to be my greatest weakness.

Thankfully, I eventually secured an internship with a $12 billion food company, which led to a full-time job after graduation. I met this company at a career conference, where two recruiters interviewed me for forty-five minutes. They saw my enthusiasm and hunger and took a chance on me, an act of mercy for which I will be forever grateful. But it was mostly luck, not skill, that landed me that internship, as I discovered a few months into the job. According to those who worked on the hiring team that year, my interviewers were inexperienced and under pressure to find people quickly at the conference. And the company didn't typically offer internships after one interview as they did with me. Had I been given a more experienced interview team, or if they had followed their company's standard two-round interview process, I probably would have been rejected.

Nevertheless, I held on to that internship offer for dear life and managed to secure a full-time offer after the summer was over. The next spring, I graduated with an overwhelming sense of gratitude that I had a job. The United States was in the middle of the worst recession since the Great Depression, and this graduate had a paycheck! But I hadn't forgotten my prior job interview struggles in school, nor did I take for granted the fact that at any time I could find myself unemployed again. I was determined to improve my interview skills because, if I was going to have a strong career, I was going to need them again and again.

Over the next five years, I worked hard to improve my interview abilities. I created comprehensive lists of possible interview questions and bucketed them into categories. I learned the purpose behind each type of question and created models for how to answer them. I joined corporate recruiting teams, attended career conferences, interviewed candidates, and made hiring decisions. I developed my own answers for each of these question categories and practiced them again and again.

In 2014, an opportunity arose for me to put my work to the test. I applied for a job as a brand manager for a $4 billion food company and was selected to fly to Denver for interviews. It was a great job and the competition was stiff. I was determined not to blow it! If I were rejected for the position, I told myself, it would be because other people were more qualified, not because I didn't put in the effort to prepare. I spent about twenty hours in the weeks leading up to the interview studying the job description, talking to people familiar with the company, preparing my stories, anticipating questions, and practicing out loud until I was blue in the face.

Interview day came and my preparation paid off. I interviewed with four marketing professionals and crushed each interview. I felt confident, relaxed, and optimistic during each conversation. Every answer felt comfortable and no question was too much for me to handle. Even though each interviewer had a different style, I could tailor my answers to each one because I had practiced so much. When I finished the day, I called my wife, Gina, and told her that I was confident an offer would come, and it did.

After that experience, I wanted to share what I had learned with others, so I started sharing my insights online. In 2015, I began posting advice articles and videos on LinkedIn, and my following started to grow. Before long, I was getting calls from people who wanted help with their interviewing skills. I hosted webinars on interviewing and took on clients who wanted help landing their next job. I still had a day job as a marketing executive, but my side gig turned into a business in 2018, Sam's Career Talk (samscareertalk.com). I have now helped hundreds of people land better jobs through my job interview frameworks.

If my journey has taught me anything, it's that job interviewing is a learned skill. Anyone with the right training and focus can dramatically improve their abilities. I continue to be amazed seeing my clients go from interview mediocrity to interview excellence in only a few weeks, sometimes even a few days! It is equally amazing how so many people don't believe this is possible. Many think that interview skills are genetically encoded traits that can't change, like eye color or height. To these people, you are either cursed or blessed forever.

The problem with this fatalistic view of interviewing is that, apart from being untrue, it leads to interview failure. If you believe you are a natural-born job interviewer, you likely won't put in the practice you need to succeed. If you believe you just don't have the skills and never will, you will retreat to self-defeat and give up before you even start. Neither approach will get you the job you want. For example, if you were to be asked the common interview question "Tell me about yourself," wouldn't it be silly to think that you could respond with exactly what the interviewer is looking for by winging it? On the other hand, wouldn't it be equally silly to assume that you could never craft an exceptional response even if you worked hard to prepare one? Of course! Not only can you deliver a great response, but you can deliver a response that is far better than that of your competition.

Interviewing is not easy. Getting competitive jobs requires going beyond surface-level interview tricks and diving deep into the mechanics of answering questions. In the pages that follow, I will show you how to answer any question that can be thrown at you, from introductory to behavioral to scenario to illegal to just plain wacky. The first four chapters focus on what to do before the interview: how to structure your preparation, how to build your confidence, how to get the right information, how to position yourself for the job, and how to most effectively practice. The subsequent chapters get into the nitty gritty on how to answer any question that can come your way. I dive into job interview questions following a winning pattern: I present a question category and then provide a simple model to help you answer the question using your own experiences. Then I demonstrate through examples what a great response looks like. This is the pattern I teach to my clients, and it works. If you follow it, you'll be ready to tackle any job interview.

I have kept the focus of this book solely on answering job interview questions because the job interview is the most consequential part of your job search. Other items, such as résumés, LinkedIn profiles, and networking, are of secondary importance and can be learned rather quickly. Many of them can even be outsourced. But not the job interview. This is the main stage event. No one can show up and do it for you, so it should command most of your time and attention throughout your search. My hope is that after reading this book, you will love job interviews. I want you to love them so much that you can't wait for your next one because you are a well-oiled job interview machine. I want you to feel deep in your bones that you can get any job you want, knowing you have mastered a skill that will serve you well for the rest of your career.

Remember my friend Heather, who came to me frustrated and angry? Two months after that initial meeting, she let me know she would no longer be needing my services. She had just signed an offer for a great new job, and Heather shed a few tears in this meeting, too. The good kind.

one.

convince your harshest critic

Believing in Yourself Changes Everything

"He hasn't sold squat," my boss said, as we picked up a thirteen-year-old kid from a street corner. We were selling newspaper subscriptions door to door. It was 1995. My boss was an ambitious entrepreneur in his twenties who, by today's standards, was probably violating a child labor law or two.

"Why do you think he hasn't sold anything?" I asked in my prepubescent voice.

"Look at him. He's slouched over and walking slowly. He's frowning and looking down at his feet. The kid looks miserable! Would you want to buy from someone like that?"

Sure enough, the teen got into the car and informed us that he hadn't sold a single subscription. He had knocked on a few doors with a reasonable amount of enthusiasm, but after being rejected a few times, he started to lose confidence. Before long, he stopped believing in his selling abilities altogether, and it showed every time he knocked on a door. He didn't believe in himself, so they didn't believe in him.

You may feel sorry for my teenaged coworker. I did. But can you blame those who rejected him? Was it their responsibility to stroke his confidence? Would you, for example, want to convince your roofer, who expresses doubts about his roofing abilities, that you know he'll build a leak-free roof over your house? Or would you want to give a pep talk to the airplane pilot on your next flight, telling her that despite coming off as inexperienced and wishy-washy when you walked on the plane, you are confident she'll get you safely home? Or how about your surgeon? I'm sure the next time you need a procedure done you'll say, "Hey, doc, I can tell by the trembling in your voice and hands that you are nervous about this surgery, but don't worry, I'm going to be fine. Now, put me to sleep and grab a scalpel!"

Of course, you wouldn't do this, because you don't believe it's your responsibility to convince people they are good at their jobs—especially when you are paying them. You'd rather move on and find someone else who is more confident. Hiring managers are no different. They don't have time to ensure candidates feel confident about their candidacy. After all, they are taking a big risk by hiring someone they know little about and hoping they will perform. They know that a bad hire not only makes their jobs harder, but it also affects how their companies view them. Their reputations are on the line! That's why lacking confidence in an interview is like putting a flashing sign on your forehead that reads, WARNING: RISKY HIRE!

If you want your interviewer to believe in you, you must first believe in yourself. You must know deep in your bones that you are an excellent candidate and that you will do a fantastic job once hired. Confidence changes everything. Hiring managers will pick up on your confidence because it will bleed through in the way you respond to questions, in the tone of your voice, in your facial expressions, even in your posture. Perhaps some people can fake confidence reasonably well, but most can't. Besides, why risk it? Why not do what it takes to be genuinely confident?

So, how do you get confident? How do you get to the point where you believe—no, that you know—you are an excellent candidate for a position? I wish there was a quick fix. I'd love to recommend a motivational speech to watch or a form of meditation to practice that would magically make you confident. Perhaps these things can give you an ego boost in the short term, but all my career-coaching experience has proven that true job interview confidence comes only on the other side of hard work. The way to feel confident that you are an excellent candidate is to be an excellent candidate, and the way to be an excellent candidate is to prepare more than anyone else.

Granted, there are a few rare souls out there who have natural confidence. They believe innately that they are the best candidate when interviewing for a job. Perhaps you are one of those people. If this is the case, then you are blessed—and cursed. Natural confidence can be an interview asset if you are well prepared but an interview liability if you aren't. Confidence without preparation comes off as arrogance, an immediate red flag that will spook your interviewer. So regardless of your natural-born confidence level, dedicated preparation is your surest way to genuine, deserved confidence. It will give you either the confidence you didn't have before, or it will validate the confidence you naturally have.

In this chapter, we'll discuss exactly how I help build confidence in my clients through preparation. I invite you to embrace three principles that will build your confidence and serve as your preparation foundation for the rest of this book:

1. Take out your mental trash.
2. Embrace the suck.
3. Commit to ten hours.

Take Out Your Mental Trash

When I was sixteen, I could eat fast food daily and feel great. In fact, I was usually hungry again after two hours. Now, at age forty-two, when I eat fast food, I pay for it for the next two days with sluggishness and headaches. No longer can I eat whatever I want and expect to feel good. Trust me, I've tried.

Eating properly became an even bigger priority for me when I started competing in triathlons. I found that if I wasn't properly feeding myself calorie-rich, easy-to-digest foods in my training sessions my body would shut down. In the triathlon world, this is called "bonking." It's when your body has nothing left to give, and no amount of willpower can summon your legs to keep running. Sometimes the lack of hydration and nutrition causes your legs to cramp up, forcing you to limp home or stop altogether. The only way to avoid bonking during a long workout session (besides consistent training, of course) is to feed your body the right nutrients consistently throughout the workout.

The same principle applies to how your brain functions when preparing for an interview. You can't feed your mind negative thoughts and expect to build interview confidence. The negative thoughts I'm talking about are the false narratives that candidates create in their minds about themselves or the interview process in general. They are partial truths or outright lies. Candidates latch onto them and repeat them to themselves until they believe them. I call them bad interview thoughts—BITs. The most common ones I see in my training are listed below and are the mental equivalent of eating fast food before a marathon. In other words, they are trash. You must get rid of them immediately. You need a clean state as you start your preparation and build your confidence.

Let's get rid of them right now by calling them out for what they are and replacing them with the truth. Here is a list of the most common BITs and the truths behind them.

BIT one: Some people are natural-born job interviewers and others aren't.

Truth: Job interviewing is a learned skill, not a born trait. If you can talk to someone and smile at the same time, you have enough natural ability to become a great job interviewer. This is not Olympic sprinting, where natural talent takes precedence over hard work; this is a job interview, where preparation and practice beat natural talent every time. Of course, a little natural-born personality never hurts, and you have plenty of it.

BIT two: Job interviewing is only for extroverts. Introverts have a disadvantage.

Truth: Job interviewing success is for those who want it bad enough. That goes for all types of "verts." The concept of introversion/extroversion was introduced by the twentieth-century psychiatrist Carl Jung. According to Jung, the main distinctions between the two types are determined by how they get their energy, not by how naturally good they are at talking to people. Extroverts get their energy from being around others, and introverts get their energy from being by themselves. Both types manifest certain strengths and weaknesses. In job interviews, introverts can come off as reserved, but they are more likely to concisely formulate answers to questions. Extroverts, on the other hand, are warm and personable but often speak before they think and can be prone to rambling. Neither type has a distinct advantage. Both types need to prepare.

Let's put aside introvert/extrovert definitions and talk about those who are shy and those who are outgoing. It's true that a naturally shy person may have to work a little bit harder to show enthusiasm, but this is easily accomplished with practice. Far more difficult is the trench work of crafting your unique story against the job description, creating your power statements, and being ready for any possible type of question thrown at you. Show me a shy person who can do that well, and I'll show you someone who will get the job. Show me an outgoing, personable person who can't, and I'll show you someone who will be shown the door after an interview.

BIT three: I wasn't qualified for the job, and that's why I didn't get it. It had nothing to do with how I interviewed.

Truth: You are qualified. You were selected to interview after they looked at your résumé and decided you were qualified. The truth is that you likely didn't get the job because you didn't interview well enough.

I admit there are some circumstances where this isn't the case. Sometimes hiring managers already know who they are going to hire but must interview other candidates to fulfill a policy requirement. There are also situations where a candidate comes highly recommended by a trusted referral (we'll talk in the next chapter about how to be that person), causing the odds to be stacked against you. But in all other situations, it's safe to assume that the reason you didn't get the job is that you didn't convince them in the interview that you are the best candidate.

Maybe that stings a little, but there is a silver lining. It means that even if you are less qualified for a job on paper, you can still get it if you prepare better and practice more than your competition. The most qualified candidate doesn't necessarily get the job; the best interviewer does.

BIT four: Most interviewers make up their minds in the first five minutes of the interview, so I don't need to prepare for the latter part of the interview.

Truth: A 2015 study lays this myth to rest. Research from *The Journal of Occupational and Organizational Psychology* showed that, in fact, 30 percent of interviewers make up their minds within the first five minutes of the interview, 52 percent make up their minds between five and fifteen minutes, and the rest make up their minds after that.

Granted, the first five minutes are clearly important, but don't count on those five minutes getting you the offer, especially for competitive jobs. If you are interviewing for a great job, count on most of your competition also making a great first impression. You'll need to do more than that to win.

BIT five: The people who will interview me are experts at job interviewing.

Truth: Hiring managers are usually not formally trained, and many have very little experience. The demands of corporate life are such that there is always a shortage of people who have time to interview, much less get trained on how to interview well. You shouldn't rely on your interviewer to be a great conversationalist, nor should you expect that all the questions will be well thought out. Don't give up your power to take control of the interview to someone who may have no idea what they're doing.

BIT six: The best thing I could do is be myself.

Truth: What does "be yourself" mean, anyway? Does it mean being the person who slept in and skipped class the other day? Or maybe that person who just yelled at their kids to go to bed? Or is it that person who binge-watched Netflix for eight hours last Saturday? It turns out we have a lot of "selves." You can be yourself when you aren't prepared, and it can still be a disaster.

Of course, I understand that this statement is meant to relax candidates. But the best way to relax is to be fully prepared. So yes, be yourself—your best prepared self.

BIT seven: I don't know what questions I will be asked beforehand, so there's really no way to prepare.

Truth: It is true that you don't know exactly what you'll be asked ahead of time. But smart candidates have a really good idea of the question *types* they will be asked. In the coming chapters, you will learn how to pick up on patterns and prepare for any question type, so nothing will be a true surprise.

BIT eight: I'm not even sure if I want this job, so it's not worth my time to prepare for the interview.

Truth: Worry about that after you have a job offer. There is no sense in stressing about a decision when there is no decision to make. If you are interested enough to interview, you should be interested enough to be all in on the interview. Leave the gut-wrenching decision-making until after you have an offer.

Recognize these BITs. Call them out for what they are. You are now on your way to having a clean interview slate and building genuine interview confidence.

Embrace the Suck

When I speak on college campuses, I can almost always count on being asked this question: "What is the one thing I can do to stand out in a job interview?" My answer is always the same. "The one thing is everything." If there were just one secret, one gimmick, one hack to getting a job offer, people would have figured it out a long time ago. But there isn't one thing. That's why the interview is thirty to sixty minutes long. You can fake it for five minutes, but not for thirty.

Students naturally don't like this response. It means more work, more hassle, and, most importantly, more confronting the things they hate doing. That's right, everyone has at least one part of interview preparation they despise. For some, it's sitting down and researching a company. For others, it's practicing their answers out loud. For me, it used to be scenario questions—the "how would you approach this situation" type of questions. I knew I wasn't good at answering them, which made focusing on them painful. So rather than addressing this clear gap in my interview skills, I focused all my time preparing for other question types that I felt more comfortable with. This worked great until I was asked a scenario question in an important interview and bombed it. From then on, I decided to do what it took to be great at scenario questions. I leaned into the pain of my incompetence and got to work. I embraced the suck.

I started with two questions:

1.   What if instead of being terrible at answering scenario questions and hating them, I was excellent at answering them and I loved them?
2.   What would it take to make that happen?

Then, I turned it into a game. I wanted to see if I could conquer these questions. I read articles and watched videos. I created lists of the most common scenario questions in my field and crafted how I would respond. I asked other professionals how they would respond to similar questions. I practiced my answers out loud on my commute to and from work. In time, I became an expert at answering them, and now I love these questions, almost to the point that other question types feel a little boring.

That is the difference between a great interviewee and everyone else. The great ones lean into the pain of their incompetence. They don't let doubt or insecurity or anything else derail them from doing what it takes to gain mastery.

Embracing the suck takes discipline. For example, do you think that I, a published author, enjoy writing? Well, most of the time I hate it. I get uncomfortable and a little fearful every time I sit down in front of my laptop to do it. Even as I write this, I'm not totally comfortable. I am staring at a half-blank screen, knowing it will stay half-blank unless I do something about it. This makes my brain want to find any possible excuse to not write—check my email, eat something, clean a toilet. Whatever it takes to not lean into the pain! And yet, when I write something good that is useful to others, I find deep fulfillment and a sense of accomplishment. So I push through the pain of my insecurity every day for the chance to find fulfillment on the other side.

But how do I discipline myself to do something so uncomfortable every day? I treat myself like a two-year-old and create basic—even juvenile—rules that I am not allowed to break. Specifically, I schedule thirty minutes a day when I have to sit down and write. I am not allowed to do anything else. If I must sit and stare blankly at the screen for a few minutes, fine, but the only thing I'm allowed to do is write. Sometimes, I get into deep flow and write for two hours, not noticing how fast the time goes by. Other times, I miserably scratch out a couple of sentences and feel like it was a total waste of time. But I don't break my rules. I keep going. This is the only way paragraphs turn into pages, which turn into chapters, which turn into a book. It's a matter of hours in front of the screen.

This may not be the method that works for you. Maybe you have the ability to lean into pain without setting up immature rules like I do. Whatever part of interview preparation sucks the most for you, if you discipline yourself and embrace the suck you can become excellent at it. And that excellence and enjoyment will give you the secret weapon of confidence in your interview.

Commit to Ten Hours

When people look back on their most defining career moments, they almost never point to a time they interviewed for a job. Rather, they point to critical decisions they made, big bets that paid off, or character-building moments. These moments are different for everyone, and yet they all have one thing in common: they would have not been possible without a successful job interview.

Nailing the interview is the accomplishment that makes all other career accomplishments possible. It's astounding, really, that a one-hour interview, or perhaps a handful of them, can be the linchpin that determines how a person will spend eight or more hours per day for the next several years or even decades. I can't think of any other professional activity where something that takes so little time has such a dramatic effect on the future.

That is why I want you to bring a preparation bazooka to the interview knife fight. I want you to be so prepared that the interview feels like a breeze compared to what you did to get there. If it's a challenging interview, you'll be glad you prepared. If your interview was easy and your preparation was overkill, you'll forgive yourself for spending five more hours than you needed to get a great job.

I'm asking you to commit to ten hours of preparation. If this sounds like a lot to you, just think about how long it takes to master piano or play sports at a competitive level or study for a math final. I'm talking about one day's worth of work or a couple of college football games or an overseas flight. This is an exceptionally small amount of time given the potential payback. When you are crushing it at a job you love for five years, you will look back on ten hours of preparation as the best time investment you made in your entire career.

Will your interview be a disaster if you don't prepare for ten hours? No. In fact, your interview might go well, but "well" might not be good enough to get you the job.

Is it possible to master interviewing in only ten hours? Absolutely. And it will put you at a distinct advantage precisely because so many people prepare for far less time. I challenge (well, force) my clients to put in a full ten hours. By the end of their preparation, they have transformed their C-minus interviews to solid A-plus interviews. And you can too.

Specifically, here's how you should structure your time:

Research: three hours

You need strong foundational knowledge of the company and position prior to going into the interview. One of the three hours should be spent reading about the company and becoming familiar with the following:

Company history: You should know where the company has been so you can better think through where the company might be going. The company website usually has a founding story section. If the company is big enough, it will have a Wikipedia page.

Company mission and values: A lot of your interview could be based on the company's stated values. If the company cares about them enough, they will be on their website.

Financials: Unless you are interviewing for a financial role, you just need the basics here. Top-line revenue, bottom-line profits, and whether those things have been growing or declining over the past few quarters and years. SEC.gov or the company website should have the company's latest annual reports. If it's a smaller, nonpublic company, you'll have to use other means to get this information (more to come on this in the next chapter). In that case, just understand the size of the company in revenue and whether they are growing or declining. More important than just the numbers is understanding *how* the company makes money. For example, Amazon is most known for its retailing website, but the majority of its profits come from Amazon Web Services (AWS), a cloud computing platform that the average person—including me—knows very little about. A lot of businesses work this way, featuring a broad array of products and services on their website while only one or two of them make most of the money.

Products and services*:* Get out and use the product or service the company offers prior to your interview. It's one of the easiest pieces of research to do and gets you familiar with the customer experience.

Current happenings*:* Companies often have hot-button issues they are dealing with in the news. It's good to know these things prior to the interview in case one comes up.

What do you do for the remaining two hours of your research? You get off your computer screen and you speak to people familiar with the company. This is the most important part of your research, by far. You'll learn more about this in the next chapter, where I discuss the power of getting inside information and how to conduct effective informational interviews.

Formulation: three hours

In the formulation phase, you sit down with the job description, apply notes from your research, and craft your responses. You start by developing seven to ten power examples: specific instances in your life that demonstrate you are perfect for the job. They are the foundation for how you answer almost all question types. This should take you about an hour. You'll spend the other two hours translating your power examples into great responses.

The process I'm describing is different from how most people prepare for interviews. Typically, candidates spend their time trying to guess all the questions they will be asked and creating answers for each unique question. This lack of focus results in a lot of wasted time and too many responses that are poorly developed and don't feature their best work.

The models I teach in the coming chapters will help you prepare excellent answers in the shortest amount of time possible. For example, in chapter 6, I'll teach you the SPAR model, which will help you tell compelling stories in response to behavioral questions. In chapter 8, I'll teach you the SEE model, which will help you answer questions about you. Each chapter makes seemingly hard questions easy. Most importantly, I will show you how to make seven to ten killer stories carry you through the entire interview.

Practice: four hours

And finally, we get to the part of preparation where most people give up—practicing your responses out loud for four hours. Many candidates fail to practice because they either feel stupid interviewing in front of a friend or themselves or they run out of time. Some believe that a lot of practice will make them sound robotic and their responses overly memorized. But those who practice find the opposite to be true. It's practice that allows responses to flow freely and allows you to improvise comfortably when needed.

Four hours is a lot of time, but the process I'll show you will make it fly by. Every time you practice a response out loud, you'll notice kinks in your answers, little awkward things you say or do that you didn't notice when you were creating your responses. As you discover these errors, you'll go back to your desk and refine your responses before practicing again. You'll follow this process of practicing, getting feedback, correcting the problem, and trying again several times until you feel comfortable with your responses. You'll spend the first hour or two doing this alone, giving yourself your own feedback as your practice. Then you'll transition to practicing in front of a friend, colleague, or career coach who can give you insights and feedback you may not have noticed on your own. We'll talk more about this in chapter 3.

What if you don't put in four hours of your practice? Will your interview be a disaster? No. In fact, it will probably be perfectly adequate—maybe even good. And that is the problem. Good is not good enough. Remember, to get the job, you must be more than good. You must be the best of all your competition.

Let me explain exactly what an interview looks like when you aren't prepared. Imagine you are interviewing for a competitive job. You enter the room and greet your interviewer with a smile. She asks you questions, and you start to discuss your experiences. At first, you feel reasonably comfortable with the answers you are giving. There aren't any long pauses or noticeably awkward moments. You notice, however, that some of your answers are taking a little longer to get to. You find yourself thinking of the answers and repeating yourself on a few occasions. Plus, there is one question you didn't anticipate, so you have to think on the fly and fumble your way through it. Not a huge deal, you think. At least you answered the other questions reasonably well. Toward the end of the interview, you ask a few questions and close by thanking her for her time. You walk out of the interview feeling like the interview went well. A solid B-plus. You also feel like you are qualified to do the job.

Do you get the job? Maybe.

Now, imagine that another candidate enters the room directly after you to interview for the same position. She is asked the same questions and evaluated in the same way. She is charismatic and has excellent experience—just like you. In fact, she is like you in nearly every way—years of experience, leadership ability, and analytical aptitude. She answers every question in a way that fully impresses the hiring manager. No rambling. No repeating herself. There is no question that she can't handle. Everything is answered in a concise and poignant way.

Does she get the job? Almost certainly.

That is the difference practice makes. It takes a candidate who has similar skills and experiences to her peers and adds a polish that sets her apart from the rest.

The Preparation Checklist

Henry Ford is alleged to have said, "Nothing is particularly hard if you divide it into small jobs." I know I've thrown a lot at you in this chapter. To make things easy for you, I've created a simple job interview checklist that breaks each part of your preparation into small, digestible pieces. Many of the models cited on the checklist aren't familiar to you yet, but they will be! I break each model down in the coming chapters. If you use this checklist every time you prepare for an interview, you can be fully confident that you are prepared.

Your Interview Preparation Checklist

Preparation Phase	Action	Completed
Research the company (3 hours)		
	Reading (1 hour)	
	Company history	✔
	Company mission and values	✔
	Financials (if available)	...
	Products and services	...
	Current events/hot buttons	...
	Speaking (2 hours)	
	2 informational interviews. Were they REAL?	...
	Did you RESEARCH the person and role beforehand?	...
	Did you EXPRESS genuine appreciation?	...
	Did you ASK the right questions?	...
	Did you LISTEN actively?	...
Formulate your responses (3 hours)		
	Power examples (3 per skill)	
	Are they relevant to the job description?	...
	Are they tangible and specific?	...

Preparation Phase	Action	Completed
Formulate your responses (3 hours) (*continued*)		
	Do they highlight your strengths?	...
	Have you created bridges where there are gaps?	...
	Opening statement	
	Does it demonstrate that you are qualified?	...
	Does it show that you get results?	...
	Does it show that you are genuinely interested in the job?	...
	5–7 behavioral responses (SPAR Model)	
	Is there a quick setup?	...
	Is there tension and drama?	...
	Do you walk through your actions sequentially?	...
	3–5 scenario responses (Home Base Model)	
	Does it start with a home base?	...
	Does it explore paths/options sufficiently?	...
	Does it either summarize learnings or pick an option?	...

Preparation Phase	Action	Completed
Formulate your responses (3 hours) (*continued*)		
	3–5 "you" responses (SEE Model)	
	Does each have a statement, explanation, and example?	...
	Prepare for land mines	
	Trap questions	...
	On-the-spot creativity questions	...
	Illegal questions	...
	Wacky questions	...
	Closing strong	
	Have you prepared 2–3 engaging and positive questions?	...
	Are you ready to resolve concerns using "I understand" and "however"?	...
	Did you ask for a timeline of next steps?	...
	Did you tell them you love them one more time?	...
Practice out loud (4 hours)		
	2 hours on your own	...
	2 hours out loud with someone else	...
Finish Line—You Are Prepared!		

So let's start learning how to master all the elements on this checklist, starting with how you can gain a major advantage through informational interviewing.

Chapter Summary

Believing in yourself is the foundation for job interview excellence. To believe you are the best candidate, you must prepare well by doing three things:

Take out your mental trash: Recognize bad interview thoughts and call them out. Then replace them with the truth. Start with a clean slate.

Embrace the suck: Find the part of interviewing that gives you the most anxiety. This is where you should focus most of your time. Discipline yourself so that you aren't afraid of any part of the interview.

Commit to ten hours of preparation:
- **three hours of research:** on paper and by talking with people familiar with the company
- **three hours of formulation:** starting with your power stories and then crafting answers to each of them
- **four hours of practice:** out loud to yourself and with someone else

Use the interview checklist to guide you through your preparation.

two.

get inside
information

Gaining an Easy Advantage

I n 1987, Ivan Boesky was sentenced to three years in prison.
Before that, he was one of Wall Street's most successful bank-
ers. He was worth $200 million—more than half a billion in
today's dollars—at his peak. With that kind of money, it's hard to
understand why someone would commit a crime to get richer, but
alas, greed knows no bounds.

His crime seemed innocent enough. He didn't steal anything or
hurt anyone, at least not in the conventional sense. All he did was
have simple conversations with his friends and make stock trades
based on what he learned from them. Those conversations and subsequent trades netted him a cool $33 million profit, creating one
of the biggest insider-trading scandals in history. Of course, in the
end, he had to pay triple that amount in fines, not to mention
spend time in the slammer.

What does the sad case of Ivan Boesky teach us? First, that
insider trading is very illegal. You can go to jail if you do it. Second,
if you ever get to half a billion dollars in net worth, quit while you

are ahead and do something else with your life. And third, having the right information at the right time (or the wrong information at the wrong time) can make an exponential difference. After all, it wasn't sheer brain power that made Ivan Boesky $33 million almost overnight, nor was it his diligent analysis of publicly available data. It was the information he had that no one else did.

I want you to be like Ivan Boesky. It's not that I want you to place illegal trades or go to jail. Rather, I want you to have his high regard for the value of information. I want you to know, as he did, that inside information can be a material advantage to you when you prepare for your next interview.

Am I really recommending that you imitate the behavior of a convicted criminal? Just hear me out. Job interviewing is not like stock trading. When preparing for a job interview, getting information from those familiar with the company is not illegal. It's not even unethical. In fact, if done the right way, it's encouraged! It's a common part of job interview preparation that can not only help you prepare but also impress those at your target company.

Think about it this way: If you were on the dating market, how would you go about identifying the right person to date? Would you leave everything up to your Instagram profile and hope that the right match will come along? Wouldn't you want to speak with someone familiar with the person before committing to a date? I would. There would be nothing illegal or unethical about doing so, which would give you an unfiltered perspective on the person without the shiny, social media veneer. More important, it will give you valuable intel to help you prepare for your first date.

You should do the same with your target company. Corporations may seem complex, but they are simply collections of individuals. If you want to study up on an individual before a date, you'll speak with people who know the person. Why should it be any different with a company?

Fortunately, there is a widely accepted method for getting inside information about a company: informational interviewing. An informational interview is a brief conversation with someone familiar with your target company in which you ask questions to learn about the company. It's effective for both getting interviews and preparing for interviews you already have.

Informational interviewing can be fun, and it's a lot less stressful than your actual interview. You control whom you speak with. You set the agenda for the conversation, and you ask the questions. The informational interviews that I've done have been low-key, enjoyable conversations that have helped me get jobs. More important, they've helped me make new friends who have stayed in my network to this day. This shouldn't just be something you only do right before you interview; it should be something you do as you are looking for a job, looking to switch jobs, or just even learning about an industry that interests you.

Do Informational Interviews Even Work?

Informational interviews can work career miracles that couldn't be worked in any other way. I've seen people use them to prepare for interviews but also to better understand industries, to get résumé advice, to get onto interview lists, and to make lifelong connections. I've personally landed several jobs through informational interviewing.

Here's one example. Earlier in my career, I was preparing for an interview with a natural foods company. I called my friend Mike. He was the only person I knew who had ever worked for that company. I figured I could get his take on the organization and his opinion on how I could do well in the interview. We had been talking for only a couple of minutes when he said, "You need to call Dave." Dave was Mike's friend and former coworker who still worked at the company. "I'll set it up," he said.

The next day, I was on the phone with Dave. "Thank you so much for speaking with me, Dave. I am interviewing with your company and just wanted to learn a little bit more about what it's like to work there."

I don't remember what questions I asked after that, but in the next twenty minutes, I learned things about the company that I couldn't have learned in any other way. I learned details about the culture. I learned which of their businesses were growing and which were declining. I learned how the marketing department functioned at the company compared to marketing departments at other companies. I learned which business unit presidents had the most power. I learned—without even asking—the personalities and traits of each of the people who were interviewing me. The information I got was a game changer for my interview preparation. I got the job and worked for the company for seven years.

I repeat, getting inside information in job interview preparation, if done the right way, is a good thing. In all my years of coaching job candidates, as well as my years of working interviewing candidates and interviewing for my own jobs, I've never seen this hurt anyone's candidacy. I've only seen it help. Not only does it help when you are preparing for the interview, but it also helps when you are trying to get an interview.

How many people do you think will take the initiative to conduct an informational interview before their formal interview? Here's a stat for you: I don't know. There is no way of knowing. But if I had to guess based on my fifteen years of experience in the workforce and in my coaching, I'd say it's far less than 20 percent. One of the reasons informational interviewing provides such an advantage is that so many people fail to do it. They believe that no one will speak with them or that it won't be productive, or they fear that it will be an awkward and uncomfortable conversation. Fine. If these people want to behave like everyone else, they must be satisfied with getting the results everyone else gets.

Informational Interviewing Should Take Most of Your Research Time

In the last chapter, I said that approximately three of your ten preparation hours should be dedicated to doing your research. Don't make the mistake of spending those hours reading about the company online. Sure, you should study the company website. You should google the latest articles on the company and check out its financials. You may even want to get some dirt on the company on Glassdoor. But you probably don't need more than a Wikipedia page's worth of information to feel confident enough to close your laptop or put down your phone and start talking with real people. When it comes to company research, talking to people is almost always better than reading. Your preparation will be incomplete if you don't interact with humans. You must go beyond electronic information and speak with people familiar with the company.

How to Get the Right People to Speak with You

If I were starting my interview preparation right now, I'd go on LinkedIn and search for the company by name. I'd then look at my network and see how many people I know who currently work for the company or who used to the work for them. If I knew them, I'd reach out directly with a note asking to speak. If I didn't know them, I'd look to see whom I know who does know them directly and ask to arrange an introduction. LinkedIn makes this easy for you by listing people as either a first connection or a second connection. A first connection means that you already know them, and LinkedIn will let you direct message them. A second connection means that you know someone who knows them. You can't direct message second connections without paying a fee, and you shouldn't anyway. The way to approach these people is through your first connections. Ask them to arrange an introduction.

LinkedIn is a valuable tool, but it's not the only tool. The principle is what's important. The principle is: do everything you can to get a warm introduction. It doesn't matter if you use social media or phone calls or handwritten notes. It doesn't matter if you find helpful people through the internet or from school or from your friend's parents. The point is that you don't want to reach out to someone cold unless you have no other choice. Introductions are always more effective than cold calls because people want to help people they know and trust. So think about past coworkers, school classmates, friends, family—they are all fair game. Start there and keep going.

How do you know you've got a great contact? Well, if you can get someone who is familiar with the company, that's pretty good.

If you can get someone who used to work for the company, even better. If it's someone who currently works for the company, even better still. If the person works for the company and the same department for which you are applying, you've hit the jackpot. The only people you don't want to speak with are those directly involved in the hiring decision or interview process, because this creates a conflict of interest for them. You don't want things to get awkward.

When you decide on the right person, reach out with a quick note requesting a brief conversation. By brief, I mean fifteen minutes. It's all you need, and it's short enough to maximize your chances of getting a yes. Who doesn't have fifteen minutes for a chance to help someone out?

In your note, tell them how much a conversation will help you and how much you appreciate the favor that they haven't yet decided to do for you. Personalize your message as much as possible. You could always email and say, "Hi, Dan, I'm interviewing with your company next week, and I'm wondering if you and I could speak for fifteen minutes about the company," but that would put Dan to sleep.

You can do better than that. I've seen people reference college sports, common interests, common friends. I've seen people reach out with offers to help them in exchange for their time. I've seen people take an interest in a project they are working on. For example, when someone reaches out to me with a comment on how my last LinkedIn post helped them, do I give it a second look? Yes. Does this mean that flattery works on me? Absolutely.

You don't need to go crazy to get someone's attention—it's still a professional call. But finding a way to connect with them other than the obvious will help you. Here's a typical example of how someone might reach out:

Hi, Dan, Sarah mentioned that you might be willing to speak with me about your company. I have an interview next week. Could I schedule time with you this week?

This is perfectly acceptable but also sort of a snooze fest. Here's how to spice up that intro to get Dan's attention and build a rapport with him right away.

Dan! We have two things in common. The first is Sarah—she is one of my favorite people. It is very kind of you to tell her you'd be willing to speak with me. The second is our love of '80s movies. I couldn't help but notice your Ferris Bueller quotes on your LinkedIn profile. I am staring at a Ferris Bueller poster in my office right now.

Fifteen minutes with you would be a huge help. I'd just like to know a little more about the company and how I can be successful there. Could I schedule fifteen minutes for us to speak sometime this week?

Who would say no to a note like this? Mean people and flakes, that's who. Everyone else should accept this request.

Make Your Informational Interviews REAL

For some people, informational interviewing is like eating vegetables. They know it's good for them. They know they'll be glad they did. But they still just can't bring themselves to take a bite and chew. One reason for hesitation is the awkwardness of reaching out, but the real reason so many people don't want to is the fear of having an awkward conversation. This is the same reason new employees don't set up thirty-minute meetings to get to know their peers and their bosses' peers (which you should do when you start your next job, by the way). The hesitation was described succinctly by one of my clients when she told me, "I want to build relationships, but I'm not big on chitchat."

Chitchat has nothing to do with it. Here is a framework to ensure that the fifteen to thirty minutes you spend on your next informational interview is a great experience for you both:

Make your informational interviews REAL.

Research

Express appreciation

Ask the right questions

Listen actively

Research: Before the call, do some research on the person you will interview. While the informational interview is meant to be informal, you should still come prepared, especially if it's with someone who currently works for the company. Treat this interview as if you are being evaluated, because you are. Do a little digging to find out about the person you are interviewing.

It shouldn't take too long. Fifteen minutes of google searching on the company and LinkedIn stalking to understand the person's background will work great. This will help you find common ground and formulate your questions ahead of time.

Express appreciation: Warm up the call by giving sincere thanks. This person is your new mentor and they will relish that title. "Thank you so much for mentoring me for a few minutes." Just hearing those words from you will start the call in an optimistic way. After all, a mentor is kind, a mentor is wise, a mentor is generous. Referring to this person as a mentor is like telling them all these things.

Another way to warm things up is to draw upon things you have in common. This could be the connection that brought you two together, or it could be something you've learned about the person in your search. In my informational interviews, I've had conversations about hometowns, summer vacations, alma maters, sports teams, music, film, Ironman races, and more.

This small talk should be brief. But it will set a friendly tone that can stay throughout your entire conversation. This person is a human who wants to help you. This conversation should be enjoyable for both parties. Make it that way.

Ask relevant questions: The interviewer is expecting you to lead the meeting. You reached out, you set up the call, you need the help, so you should drive the conversation. How do you know what questions to ask? Start by avoiding the following questions:

- *Suck-up questions:* These are questions that you ask because you want to appear impressive. You don't really care about the answer to these questions but are trying to gain points by showing how smart you are. For example, "I read on your annual report that you had to restate your net income last year. Can you describe why?" Overly smart interview questions like this can get you into trouble.

Not only will the interviewee not know the answer to this question, they will see that you are trying to impress them.

- *Nonapplicable questions:* These questions are those that the interviewee is not qualified to answer or that have nothing to do with the job you are interested in. Asking a finance person about a new marketing strategy, for example, probably makes the person uncomfortable and feel put on the spot.
- *Selfish questions:* These are questions you probably want to know the answers to, but they're tacky to ask. Questions about how often pay raises occur or how much vacation is okay to take in the first year should be held until you've signed your offer.

What do good questions look like?

A good question has three elements. First, it's something that you are genuinely interested in. Second, it applies to the job description. Third, it is something that the person is uniquely qualified to answer. Sticking to these parameters will eliminate a lot of bad questions.

Here are some examples:

- What is your background? I'd love to hear about your career path and how you got to where you are.
- What is the culture like at the company and in your department?
- How does someone really excel at your company? What are your most successful employees like?
- What are some of the biggest challenges you are currently facing as an organization?

- Do you have any advice on how I can be successful during the interview process?

These questions are general. You can get even more specific if you want. Just remember the three critical elements of a great question: genuine interest, applicability, and qualification. Stick to these three parameters and you won't go wrong.

Listen actively: This is what gives your interview the potential to be productive for both parties. Active listening helps you know if the person you are interviewing is in a hurry or if they are enjoying the interview so much that they want to talk for another thirty minutes. An active listener looks for cues, asks follow-up questions, takes the conversation to a place that feels natural, and, when needed, shuts up and ends the call. Active listeners also validate the person on the other side of the phone, often restating or summarizing their responses to prove that they are listening.

Closing Your Interview

Once you have a REAL interview with someone and your time is up, thank them again. But don't just thank them—thank them specifically. Tell them exactly what you learned from them and why it will be so helpful to you.

What you do next depends on your active listening. How did the conversation go? Was this person cold or warm? How good was your friendship before the call and how good is it now? Your answer to these questions determines how forward you should be. If you feel lucky, you could ask the person to put in a good word for you during the interview process. If you don't yet have an interview, you could ask if they would pull strings to get you on the interview list. If you want to go a little softer, you could say that any help they could give you along your journey would be very much appreciated.

Regardless of the path you choose, you should never leave the interview without asking this question: "Is there anyone else you can think of that I should speak with?" This magical question can open more doors for you. In fact, that question alone has made many of my informational interviews worth it—even the ones I felt weren't going anywhere.

Chapter Summary

Informational interviewing is your interview prep secret weapon. It's legal and ethical inside information that will give you an advantage over your competition.

You should spend most of your two hours of preparation talking to people instead of reading about the company online.

Never cold-call unless you absolutely have to. Use your network and your creativity to get a warm introduction.

When conducting an informational interview, make it REAL.

- Research: read about the company and the person as you formulate your questions.
- Express sincere appreciation by thanking your new friend and mentor.
- Ask relevant questions that you are genuinely interested in, that pertain to the job description, and that your contact is uniquely qualified to answer.

- Listen actively; make the conversation enjoyable and productive by validating responses and reading the room.

Never leave the conversation without asking, "Is there anyone else you can think of whom I should speak with?"

Preparation Checklist Progress

Speaking (2 hours)	
2 informational interviews. Were they REAL?	✔
Did you RESEARCH the person and role beforehand?	✔
Did you EXPRESS genuine appreciation?	✔
Did you ASK the right questions?	✔
Did you LISTEN actively?	✔

three.
craft power examples
Positioning Yourself for the Job

Austin Church was a medical doctor turned entrepreneur. Born in 1877 and orphaned as a child, Church found a way to graduate from high school and put himself through Yale medical school. After ten years of practicing medicine, he switched careers. Apparently, Church had been experimenting in his kitchen in his spare time, trying to find a yeast substitute that could make bread rise. He found the solution when he combined sodium carbonate with carbon dioxide to form sodium bicarbonate, also known as baking soda. Church partnered with his brother-in-law John Dwight to bring to market the first commercially available baking soda, making it in Dwight's farmhouse kitchen. Such were the humble beginnings of the Arm & Hammer baking soda brand.

Arm & Hammer's sales grew for decades, making baked goods across America light and fluffy. Then, in the 1960s, the brand reached market saturation and sales stalled at around $16 million per year. This could have been the beginning of a slow decline for the brand, full of budget cuts and "milk it for cash" strategies. But then, in a stroke of marketing genius, the company found a way forward. They came up with a marketing campaign promoting the idea that Arm & Hammer baking soda could control odors. They repackaged the product from a bag to a box and told consumers to buy three of them. "Box one is for my bath," one television advertisement said. "Box two is for my freezer, so ice cream and ice cubes won't taste funny." It concluded with, "Box three deodorizes my refrigerator. With melons and potato salad, I need it!" The brand also recommended that the boxes be replaced monthly.

The campaign was a wild success. Within a year, more than half of American refrigerators contained a box of Arm & Hammer baking soda and, between 1970 and 1995, brand sales grew 25 percent per year to more than $300 million. Today, Church and Dwight, the parent company of the Arm & Hammer brand, brings in more than $4 billion in revenue and has found a way to market its baking soda in products ranging from laundry detergent to toothpaste to nasal spray.

The Arm & Hammer story is a classic example of brand positioning. Rather than come up with a completely new product when sales stalled, the Arm & Hammer team repositioned their current product for a new application, allowing consumers to view it in a different way and ushering in new avenues of growth.

As a food marketing executive, I've observed the power of brand positioning throughout my career. I'm fascinated with how easily consumers can change their minds about a product with just a few tweaks to the message. For example, what is the difference between high-quality raw beef and steak tartare? Not much, other than a fancy French name and some spices! And yet that small change in messaging makes many people believe that one will make you sick and the other is a delicacy. Or what's the difference between cold soup and gazpacho? Again, nothing, yet one sounds gross and the other sounds tasty, according to some people. Finally, what is the difference between bacon and pancakes and a ham sandwich? Very little nutritionally, but somewhere along the way, someone decided that one should be eaten for breakfast and the other for lunch, and we all now accept it as correct.

Positioning isn't merely for food products. It's everywhere! It surrounds us in fashion, politics, business, education, parenting, religion, and even science. Those who know how to leverage its power often wind up getting what they want.

One of my favorite examples of political positioning is from the 1984 presidential debate between Ronald Reagan and Walter Mondale. Reagan was running for a second term. He was seventy-three years old, the oldest candidate in presidential history at that time, and seventeen years older than Mondale. In the debate, the moderator asked Reagan, "You already are the oldest president in history and some of your staff say you are tired after your recent encounter with Mr. Mondale. I recall that President Kennedy had to go days on end with very little sleep during the Cuban Missile Crisis. Is there any doubt in your mind that you would be able to function in such circumstances?" Without skipping a beat, Reagan replied, "Not at all . . . and I want you to know that also, I will not make age an issue in this campaign. I am not going to exploit, for political purposes, my opponent's youth and inexperience."

Point Reagan! In a beautiful stroke of repositioning, he took a potential negative about his candidacy and turned his age into a towering strength. The audience howled. The moderator loved it. Even Mondale couldn't keep a straight face. Ronald Reagan demonstrated in his response exactly why he was great for the job by positioning his age as meaning experience and wisdom.

Positioning should play a critical role in your next job interview. As part of your preparation, you must practice positioning yourself by carefully studying the job description, developing your power examples, and planning how you overcome gaps in your skills and experiences. I'm going to show you how to do it in this chapter.

Leverage the Job Description

How many consumers read the user manual before using a recently purchased product? I've seen numbers as high as 75 percent and as low as 25 percent. I suppose no one truly knows, but my guess is the number is more in the 25 percent range—and for good reason. Some user manuals are so dense and boring that it's better to simply ask YouTube how to work your new product. Other manuals, like IKEA furniture assembly instructions, show a series of stick figures doing seemingly random things without any explanatory words, leaving consumers frustrated when they find themselves holding two extra screws and a wooden dowel at the end of their project. In other words, consumers think manuals are the worst, and they're right.

Job descriptions are like instruction manuals except they aren't the worst. In fact, a job description is a gold mine—a document that tells you exactly how to prepare for the interview by listing the skills required for the job. It's the ultimate cheat sheet. It tells you critical details about the company, the specific position, and what the perfect candidate looks like. Some may also give a pay range and list the benefits and perks the company offers. If a company makes the effort to post a job, they typically make sure to include a clear and accurate job description that can serve as a blueprint for your interview preparation.

Unfortunately, many job candidates treat a job description like a user manual, as a useless document to be quickly looked over and then discarded. From my observation, less than half of job candidates use the job description as a core part of their preparation. What a shame! If you carefully study the job description, you can easily detect what skills are required for the job and thus what types of questions you will be asked. Let's look at a couple of job descriptions and I'll show you what I mean.

Suppose you are a home-building professional with four years of post-college work experience building homes. You also have a bachelor's degree in construction management. You come across a job description that looks interesting to you.

Here's what the opening section says:

Renovations, Inc., is on the lookout for a Project Manager, Store Construction to join our Store Design and Construction team to support and lead every facet of opening a new store or renovating and refreshing existing locations, from design development, bidding, permitting, construction management to turnover of the space. If you love airline miles and weaving your way through some of the nation's coolest neighborhoods, malls, and lifestyle centers, then this active, fast-paced job may be just for you. Our ideal person is experienced and sophisticated in all things site and vendor management (think: timeline management, budget, and quality control) and will be a key collaborator across the company for our new store development projects. Sound like your cup of tea (or yerba maté or coffee)? Then read on!

In this brief overview, you now know some critical details about the position, like:

- It requires a lot of travel.
- It focuses on commercial properties, not residences, which is different from your experience.
- It requires project and timeline management skills.
- It requires you not only to build new stores but also to renovate existing stores.
- It requires you to lead projects from beginning to end, not just a specific part.

The next sections of the job description dive deeper into the job responsibilities and requirements:

What You'll Do

Manage project buildouts in collaboration with internal stakeholders and external vendors to ensure that each store is designed within budget and optimized for seamless operations

Review architectural plans, lease exhibits, shop drawings, various vendor proposals, and other documentation related to the design development and construction processes

Review feasibility reports and LOIs and advise the Warby Parker Store Design and Construction leadership team on base building conditions, layouts, dimensions, and engineering requirements

Prepare bid packages for GCs, manage RFis and shop drawing approvals, review and approve materials quotes, and level and negotiate GC bids

Facilitate weekly project meetings with GCs, designers, architects, OFi vendors, and landlords as needed

Perform thorough walk-throughs for each project and create detailed punch list reports

Execute and manage the project closeout process involving all documentation and coordination for GCs, OFi vendors, and Warby Parker operations, facilities, and finance teams

Who You Are

Equipped with 3-5 years of experience in retail construction project management

Unflappable in managing multiple projects and budgets at once

Experienced in the luxury or specialty retail store development industry

Armed with strong analytical, scheduling, and computer skill sets

An expertly organized person with uncharted attention to detail (almost—almost!—to a fault)

An excellent communicator with negotiation skills that could resolve geopolitical conflicts

A natural leader experienced in vendor management and in facilitating large, diverse teams of internal and external partners

An expert in reviewing and interpreting architectural drawings and construction site management

A frequent flier prepared to travel about 50 percent of the time for store openings and buildouts

Proficient in Microsoft Excel, Word, PowerPoint, and Google Workspace

Option for the role to be NYC-based or remote

Not on the Office of Inspector General's List of Excluded Individuals/Entities (LEIE)

Extra Credit

A bachelor's degree related to project management

Design or engineering project management experience

Background in budget development for executive-level approval

Working knowledge of project management software such as PlanGrid and MS Project

I'm not a construction management professional, but I can easily pick out the skills required for a position like this and thus the question types I'd likely be asked. I have boiled them down to five critical areas. These will almost certainly be the focus areas of your interview questions:

1. Ability to manage a lot of variables and complexity in a high-stakes project environment
2. Ability to lead and work well with other stakeholders in an organization
3. Technical construction and project management skills
4. Financial analysis skills to prepare and review bids and meet budgets
5. Three to five years of experience, ideally in commercial/retail development

Let's look at another example. Suppose you are graduating from college with a degree in marketing in a couple of months. You are looking for your first real job out of school and have a strong interest in social media. As you browse LinkedIn, you come across this description:

Summary of Responsibilities

Awesome Brands, Inc., is looking for a talented social media professional to help us manage and grow our social media portfolio across our portfolio of brands. This role will be responsible for charting, creating, and posting all brand content on Facebook, Twitter, LinkedIn, YouTube, TikTok, Instagram, and blogs, as well as helping to coordinate execution and reporting for our multiple marketing initiatives. This role will require being in the field and traveling, so reliable transportation is required. We are looking for a social media addict who lives, eats, and breathes on all the popular platforms; personally and professionally.

Essential Functions

Plan, create, develop, and maintain all content (including original text, images, and video) for our Facebook, Instagram, Twitter, YouTube, Blogs, LinkedIn, and other websites or social media outlets within brand standards

Collaborate with marketing team to develop social media campaigns

Implement daily social media content updates

Stay up to date on the latest social media best practices and technologies

Set up and optimize company pages within each platform to increase the visibility of the company's social content

Build and monitor engagement

Capture and analyze the appropriate social data/metrics and social media best practices

Moderate and leverage user-generated content

Vet and manage influencer relationships

Monitor and interact daily with comments and messages, responding to customer inquiries and concerns

Create editorial calendars and syndication schedules

Attend community events and spend time in the field getting pictures and videos, interacting with customers, and acting as a representative of our brands

Other duties as necessary

Required Experience

BA in Communications, Digital Media, or Marketing preferred

Previous experience managing a professional social media brand

Extensive knowledge of online communication mediums such as Facebook, Twitter, blogs, YouTube, LinkedIn, Instagram, TikTok

Ability to develop and implement social media strategy

Background in innovative ideas and content creativity, presenting new ways to interact with and increase customer base

Must possess excellent organizational skills

Intermediate to advanced proficiency in the following:

Microsoft Office

Microsoft Project

Social media apps

Basic HTML

Photoshop

Physical Requirements

This position requires sitting, standing, bending, kneeling, or lifting up to 25 pounds.

Travel to company events will be required to feature on our social media.

Working Conditions

Schedule flexibility including nights and weekends where necessary

Comply with the brands and company uniform and hygiene standards

Fun, dynamic environment

In reading this job description, it's clear what skills will be required. They are:

1. Familiarity and expertise with multiple social media platforms, especially skills gained by posting content for other businesses
2. Ability to work well with the marketing team to ensure they are getting what they need and to build relationships with external stakeholders, such as social media influencers
3. Ability to stay up to date on social media trends
4. Analytical ability to report and explain marketing performance
5. Organization ability to plan events and coordinate marketing initiatives

These two job descriptions I've provided as examples may not be relevant to your career. That's okay. All job descriptions follow a similar pattern. The process of picking out the skills required and the types of questions you'll be asked is the same, regardless of industry, function, or level. The key is not to ignore the job description. Doing so is the equivalent of taking an open-book test without opening the book.

Build Your Power Examples

The next step after you've developed your list of skills is to create your power examples. These are instances in your past when you have successfully demonstrated the skills listed in the job description. These examples should be your best stuff, your highlight reel, the things you can't wait to share with the interviewer because they make you look like the high performer you are. These power examples will serve as the foundation for how you craft your interview responses.

Your power examples need three things to be effective. First, they should be directly relevant to the job description. They won't do you any good if you never get asked about them, and you're likely to be asked only questions that are related to the skills they are trying to assess. Second, they should be tangible and specific. You won't be able to develop robust responses if your examples are merely principles or ideas. Third, they should make you the hero. They won't be as effective if they don't make you look like a rock star.

Your power examples can be merely rough sketches. Don't worry about phrasing your power examples perfectly at this stage in your preparation. I'll teach you later in the book how to turn them into engaging, compelling responses to a diverse set of questions. The key here is to get them down on paper.

You should aim to have three power examples for every skill you identify in the job description. This will give you flexibility in the interview because questions are often phrased in different ways. For example, an interviewer assessing your collaboration skills could ask how you have demonstrated collaboration in a group setting, or she could ask how you have dealt with a difficult coworker. Also, pay particular attention to the skills listed at the top of the job description because required skills are typically written in descending order, with those they care most about at the top.

Here's a list of potential skills, with three power examples for each skill:

Skill: analytical ability
Power examples:

- Created a tool in Excel that helped my department manage inventory that's still in use today
- Developed a matrix showing our highest and lowest sales customers and compared it to our highest and lowest profit customers to improve our customer mix
- Analyzed what the best flavors were in our product lineup based on several variables of consumer feedback

Skill: collaboration
Power examples:

- Mediated group discord during a critical school project when we faced a deadline
- Built a relationship with a coworker who saw me as a threat at first
- Turned around an angry customer who called in upset and made her a happy one

Skill: social media prowess

Power examples:

- Grew the campus activities accounts on Facebook, Instagram, and Twitter
- Took extra classes on social media performance and placed in the top 10 percent of my class
- Helped several local businesses establish and grow their accounts

Sales skills

Power examples:

- Grew customers by 50 percent by creating advertising campaigns based on consumer insights
- Achieved top salesperson of the month three times in one year
- Overcame objections with my boss and the entire team to push through my new product initiative

Project management skills

Power examples:

- Managed our booth at the biggest trade show of the year in our industry
- Led student consulting project with five other students that helped a local restaurant be more efficient
- Launched a new website within three months of joining the company and got buy-in from ten critical stakeholders

That's it—it's that simple at this stage of your preparation. You don't need a fully built story or specific numbers yet; you'll craft that later. All you need now is a list of tangible things that apply to the job and make you look like a rock star.

Bridge Your Gaps

I have a LinkedIn connection who is a borderline troll. He frequently comments on others' career posts on LinkedIn, repeating the same idea again and again. His message is that there is an inconsistency in the hiring process—an "employment catch-22" as he calls it. It's the notion that candidates need experience to get a certain job but can't get said experience without such a job. He is painfully repetitive and more than a little annoying in his approach, but he has a point. You need to get experience to prove you have experience.

You may run into the same challenge when creating power examples for your next interview. Some of your experiences may not line up well with the job you seek. Maybe you are trying to switch careers or functions. Perhaps you applied for a job because you want new experiences. Regardless of how amazing your previous experience is, chances are there is something in the description for which you don't have experience. This can make developing directly relevant power examples a unique challenge.

This problem is common and solvable. While some candidates have experience that is naturally a better fit for a position than others, no candidate is a 100 percent perfect match. Employers recognize this. Just as you know that the perfect job with the perfect salary and perfect work-life balance doesn't exist, employers know that there is no such thing as the perfect employee with the perfect experience at the perfect, low price. They know that, if an employee is 100 percent qualified for the job, they are likely over-qualified. And, while my LinkedIn friend raises a good point about the "employment catch-22," all of us would be unemployed if it always held true. And remember, you have been selected to interview, so they are interested in what you have to offer.

That said, you still need to position yourself and your experience in the best possible way, even if some of your experience doesn't exactly match. You do this through bridging. This is a technique where you take a seemingly unrelated experience and make it relevant to the desired skill listed in the job description.

For example, I have a friend who interviewed for a marketing position with Disney while he was in business school. He was studying marketing in school, but before that, he had earned a PhD in history—a great accomplishment for sure but not exactly typical experience for a competitive marketing job. He knew this would come up in the interview, so he needed to bridge his experience. He thought about how his expertise in history applied to marketing and realized that his interest in history stemmed from a desire to better understand human behavior, which was at the core of marketing. He was able to explain this in the interview, and together with answering other questions successfully, he landed the position.

I have had to use bridging for every job interview I've been in. When I interviewed for a role selling radio ads, I had some experience selling ads for newspapers, but I was completely unfamiliar with radio, so I had to take the skills I used selling one medium and translate them to selling another medium. When I interviewed for a position as a communications analyst for a government IT project, I knew nothing about government contracts or systems implementations, but I did know how to communicate my ideas effectively, so I sent my potential boss some samples of my writing that I felt were relevant. Those samples worked wonders. It gave him the confidence that I could think critically and that I would pick up industry-specific skills over time. When I interviewed for an executive position at a small food company, they were skeptical that I could do the job because all my previous experience had been with large corporations, so I told them about a project I did at one of my big companies where I ran a small brand with very few resources. That story gave them confidence that I could operate in a small-company environment.

Let's look at a hypothetical example. Suppose you are interviewing for a position selling software and are in the middle of developing your power examples, but all your sales experience is in selling insurance. You know in the interview you will have a gap around your lack of experience with technical products. In this case, you want to think about how your experience would apply to technology. Perhaps you were the best in your office at using insurance software? Maybe you have been building out your skills in software by taking online courses when you aren't at work. Or maybe selling insurance requires a level of technical ability and attention to detail that is a perfect fit for software sales. All these bridging examples would work well.

But what if you don't have any sales experience but are great with technology? Easy, just bridge the other way. Think about times when you have sold anything to anyone, even an idea. Walk your interviewer through the process of how you converted someone to your way of thinking. Discuss a time when you went above and beyond to make sure someone was completely satisfied. Or highlight what you are doing right now to improve your ability to sell.

If you are struggling with a gap in your experience, don't let it discourage you as you develop your power examples. Remember, they are looking for you to give them reasons to hire you, so do it; give them reasons through power examples. Some of those examples will come easily, and others will require bridging. Either way, your examples must make it easy for them to connect the dots. The more your power examples spoon-feed them exactly why you are the best option, the better.

Chapter Summary

Positioning is an essential job interview skill and a critical focus of your preparation.

You start the positioning process by studying the job description and identifying the skills and experiences required for the job, paying special attention to the first three to five skills or experiences listed.

Next, you create at least three power examples for each skill you identify. Power examples are instances where you demonstrated those skills. Strong power examples:

- are relevant to the job description; and
- are tangible and specific.

In cases where your experience isn't a direct match with the required skills, bridge your skills by taking seemingly unrelated experiences and making them applicable to the job description.

Preparation Checklist Progress

Power examples (3 per skill)	
Are they relevant to the job description?	✔
Are they tangible and specific?	✔
Do they highlight your strengths?	✔
Have you created bridges where there are gaps?	✔

four.

practice
with humans

Accelerating Your Performance

When I was nineteen, I needed to learn Portuguese fast. I had signed up for a two-year missionary assignment in Brazil for my church, and I would have to preach to Brazilians in their native tongue. I was both excited and terrified by this assignment. Never had I lived in a foreign country, and my language-learning ability was limited to two years of high school Spanish. My older brother, having completed a similar assignment in Chile a few years earlier, gave me some counterintuitive advice on how to learn a new language quickly. "Just speak it," he said. "If you want to learn the language fast, speak it."

Now, I love my brother, but this seemed like terrible advice. How was I supposed to speak a language I didn't, well, speak? I politely listened to his advice and filed it away in the "I'll probably never do that" space in my mind. A couple of months later, off I went to Brazil. We missionaries always traveled in pairs, and I was assigned to be with another American. Thank goodness! He had been in Brazil for nearly two years and spoke Portuguese fluently.

I considered it a huge stroke of luck to have been given an American instead of a Brazilian for a companion so that I could at least speak English to him.

My first couple of months in Brazil were among the most difficult in my entire life as I scrambled to adjust to a new climate, new food, and new culture. I walked around the streets of São Paulo trying to speak with strangers, and no one could understand me. I sat in people's living rooms attempting to teach them something and saw pity in their eyes as they watched me struggle. My brain hurt from mentally translating every English word into Portuguese, one by one. There were some days when I wanted to crawl into a cave and cease to exist. The only respite I got was when I was alone with my companion because then we could at least speak English.

Then, three months into my mission, I was assigned another companion—a native. He didn't speak a lick of English, so if we wanted to communicate, it had to be in Portuguese. It was difficult at first, but something amazing happened as time went on. The language started to click for me. Soon, I was speaking in Portuguese without directly having to translate it one word at a time. I even started to dream in Portuguese. Within a couple more months, I was fluent. After a year, I spoke so well that many Brazilians I met couldn't tell I was American.

That's when I realized the wisdom in my brother's advice. Living with a native forced me to speak the language, and that's what helped me pick it up. All the pain and frustration I experienced paid off.

Learning to interview works the same way. The best way to master it is to do it. The discomfort and frustration wrought by practicing job interviews is exactly what you need to rapidly improve.

In this chapter, I'll cover the most difficult and most overlooked part of job interview preparation and teach you how to practice so you can interview at your best.

The Problem with "Good" Candidates

Julie was a strong candidate for a position on my team, having come highly recommended by one of our board members. After a successful conversation over the phone, I decided to interview her, so we brought her in a couple of weeks later and interviewed her as a team. We asked her some standard questions and she had solid answers. She was charming and pleasant. All her answers were appropriate and acceptable to us. After the interview, my team and I were fully prepared to give Julie an offer.

That is, until our recruiter asked us to interview Kim, who was charming and pleasant, just like Julie. She had similar levels of experience and aptitude. But Kim's answers weren't merely acceptable; they were outstanding. She had stories that clearly demonstrated her ability to do the job well. She had great ideas about how to fulfill her future role. She had insightful questions that were directly applicable to the job. Kim got the offer, of course. It wasn't that Julie was bad. It's just that Kim was better.

I've personally been on the winning and losing side of this equation in my career. It still stings when I remember losing a job to a schoolmate because she wanted the job more than I did and therefore prepared harder. On paper, we were basically equal, with similar experience and similar schooling. But she hustled more and won.

Another time, later in my career, I was the winner. I wanted a job so badly that I was willing to put in any amount of preparation necessary to get it. I knew it was impossible to guarantee that I'd be *the* best interviewee because I didn't know my competition. But I also knew that I could prepare to be at *my* best and have no regrets, so I prepared accordingly, nailed the interview, and got the offer. It was only after this ordeal that I found out one of my coworkers had interviewed for the exact same position and that I had beaten him out. This coworker was a great friend. We had been hired at our current company at the same time in the same function. We had basically the same education and the same marketing training. He was talented, smart, charismatic, and fun. The whole package! In fact, I was a bit surprised that I had gotten the offer instead of him.

When we finally realized we had been competing for the same job, we compared notes on the interview process. That's when I learned that he had not prepared nearly as much as I had. He had gotten busy with work and didn't practice. He said that he felt like his interview was "good, not great." He mentioned a couple of awkward moments and a couple of questions that he didn't expect and therefore hadn't prepared for. I realized after our conversation that I had gotten the job instead of him not because I was the better natural candidate with more innate talent, but simply because I had outhustled him.

This scenario plays out again and again at companies all over the world, every day. Good candidates finish job interviews feeling as if they gave perfectly acceptable performances that merit an offer, only to be disappointed when they aren't offered the job. To compound the disappointment, they rarely get feedback from their target company on why no offer came.

This has happened to me personally. Has it happened to you? If so, I'll give you the feedback that that company would have given you had they had more time, cared more, and weren't afraid of getting sued. The feedback is this: someone else interviewed better than you.

There's nothing wrong with being a "good" candidate or having a "good" interview, other than the fact that it may not get you the job you want. To be precise, being good in the interview will give you a good chance of getting the job; being great in the interview will give you a great chance of getting the job; but being the best interviewee will give you the best chance of getting the job. This is a competition, people!

Practice Is Your Secret Weapon

Companies will pick the best candidate for the job, and the best candidate in their eyes is almost always the one who had the best interview. You become the best interviewee with practice. One reason practicing can make you the best candidate is that so many other candidates fail to do it. I've coached a lot of people who have failed to put in the time to practice, and it usually shows. I don't blame people for failing to practice. I won't sugarcoat it: practice is the hardest part of job interview preparation, and it is where most people stop. Here are the most common reasons:

It's time-consuming: In fact, it's the most time-consuming part of your preparation. Four of your ten hours should be dedicated to it. It's so much easier to research the company, prepare your responses, run through them in your head, and think, "I'll be fine." Maybe you will, but you will only know for sure if you practice.

It's uncomfortable: Practice is the part of your preparation that feels the most awkward because it has a way of uncovering weaknesses quickly. But the awkwardness is good because it motivates you to fix the areas that need to be fixed. For example, if you are asked in a mock interview about your analytical ability and you fumble through your answer, the awkwardness you feel will be the catalyst for you to address a weakness that needs attention. No other interview prep method works quite as effectively as a little bit of pain.

Candidates don't believe it will help: Many people believe that practice takes away the "be yourself" factor. They think, if they practice too much they'll sound robotic and not natural. The opposite is true. The mastery gained through practice is what will give you the ability to go off script and improvise a little because you are so familiar with the material.

Despite these understandable reservations, practice is so worth it! If you practice, you'll have a significant advantage over other candidates. Just as I can empathize with those who don't put in the practice, I've never met anyone who regretted practicing. It has not only helped my clients get the jobs they wanted, but it has given them a confidence and a polish that they can take with them for future job interview opportunities. It's the magic ingredient that takes them to the next level. Once they are sold on the idea that they need to practice, they are never the same.

Jim Rohn said, "Success is nothing more than a few simple disciplines, practiced every day." The principles in this book are simple, but you must practice them to extract their full value. Of course, some practice is more effective than others, so in this next section, I'll teach you how to use your time.

Start with a read-through.

Growing up, I was involved in live theater and acted in several productions. In the initial stages of preparing for a play, it's common for the cast to do a read-through. This is when the members read the script from beginning to end together. A full read-through allows the cast to see how the script sounds out loud and how the various parts of the play work together. It's a critical part of the preparation process that helps to form a cohesive performance.

Similarly, the beginning of your interview practice should start with a read-through. After you have written down your responses, or at least a rough structure based on the techniques you'll learn in this book, read them out loud in full sentences as if an interviewer had asked you a question. As you do this, you'll be shocked at how different some of your responses feel than what you originally imagined. Some sentences will work well together, and others just won't sound right in your mind. If this happens to you, you'll know you are improving. Just think how much pain you are saving yourself in the actual interview!

Once you determine which parts of your responses don't sound right, go back to your written responses and make changes. Then, read them again. Do this until it feels right.

Go "off book."

Once you feel comfortable with the flow and feel of your responses, it's time to go "off book." This is another theater term that means you are ready to ditch the script and speak from memory. Now you get to create the wiring in your brain that will allow you to give full responses without having to refer to your notes. It's an iterative process of imagining that you are being asked questions and responding to them.

This doesn't have to be drudgery. I've found the best time for me to memorize my lines is while I'm on a walk or when I'm in the car while commuting. This whole process shouldn't take more than an hour or two. Now you're ready for the part of preparation that will really move the needle: the dress rehearsal.

Your Dress Rehearsal

An essential part of any production is a dress rehearsal a day or two before the show. This is just like the real play but without the audience. If something goes wrong in a dress rehearsal, the cast must figure it out just as if the audience were there. But why? Why make the cast run through all their lines as if there were people in the audience when they already know them? Why make them put on makeup and costumes and run through lines that they've already run through several times before? Why make the sound and lighting crew go through all their transitions when they already know them in their heads? Because only by simulating the actual production with all its intricacies does the director know if the production is truly ready for the public. Dress rehearsals work amazingly well. It's embarrassing when things go wrong, but not nearly as embarrassing as it would have been if an audience had been present. Plus, that embarrassment is a great motivator to fix the problem for prime time.

When it comes to interview preparation, your dress rehearsal is a mock interview. It's your opportunity to know if you are truly ready because you've simulated the actual experience and you know what it's like. I've done hundreds of mock interviews, and they increase interview performance more effectively than any technique I've ever seen. I'm often astounded at how much my clients improve their skills from the first mock interview to the second I do with them. When people know they will have to perform, they often deliver.

But the rehearsal must be done right to be effective. Here are some guidelines to ensure that you have a successful mock interview:

Get an interviewer who will take it seriously: An experienced career coach will give you the best results because they have seen enough candidates and know what to look for. They'll be able to go beyond delivery and give you feedback on how you've structured your answers. They can also recommend revisions that will be helpful. But if you don't want to pay the money, you can still get great results by asking a friend or family member or school counselor to give you a mock interview. The improvement mostly comes from within you anyway because you'll be the most acutely aware of your mistakes. Whomever you ask, just make sure they take it seriously.

Don't break character: It's highly tempting to frequently stop in the middle of mock interviews to correct yourself or clarify things. After all, it's all fake anyway. But resist this temptation. If you feel yourself rambling during one of your responses and want to start over, imagine that you are in the actual interview and find a way out. Feeling the discomfort of rambling in your mock interview will fuel the motivation to not ramble in your real one.

Hold all feedback to the end: Ask your interviewer to take notes along the way, but don't pause after each question to get feedback. No real interview works like that, so your mock interview shouldn't either.

Get honest, candid feedback: Ask your interviewer to give you feedback on everything. The way you structured your answers, your tone, your posture, your facial expressions. Everything. I had a mock interviewer give me feedback once that my arms were crossed the whole time in my interview, and because of that, he thought I seemed disengaged from the interview, which a real interviewer might not like. Another mock interviewer didn't like it when my working style was like that of a "chameleon," which I took to mean that I was adaptable. He said that in his experience, that term could mean that you changed based on the way the wind blew and that you didn't have a lot of your own principles. Who knew?

Do two mock interviews: It's best to do two forty-five-minute mock interviews, with fifteen minutes of feedback at the end, for a total of two hours of preparation. You could always do more, but I've found that two is the magic number that will give you the most improvement. Candidates are usually pretty close to their peak after two mock interviews, as long as they've followed all the other preparation steps. If you can't do two, one is still very valuable and strongly recommended.

Allow your interviewer to develop the questions: Part of simulating the actual interview experience is not knowing exactly what questions you'll be asked. So, when preparing your interviewer, show them the job description and give them a general sense of question types, but let the interviewer come up with the questions.

Chapter Summary

It's often not enough to have a "good" interview. To secure the offer, you have to have a better interview than everyone else.

Practice is the secret weapon to being better than your competition because your competition doesn't want to practice.

Your four hours of practice should include:

- A read-through where you take your written response structure and verbalize it to see how it sounds.
- An "off-book" phase where you memorize your written responses.
- A dress rehearsal where you simulate the real interview by
- getting an interviewer who will take it seriously;
- not breaking character;
- holding feedback until the end;
- getting honest, candid feedback;
- doing two mock interviews (but no less than one); and
- allowing your interviewer to develop questions.

Preparation Checklist Progress

2 hours on your own	✔
2 hours out loud with someone else	✔

five.

start with momentum

Owning the First Question

My first job interview out of college was a painful experience. Literally painful. I got appendicitis the day before
my interview.

I was applying for my first real job, as an analyst for a consulting
firm based in Washington, DC. This company was the real corporate deal. It had $3 billion in annual revenue, an A-list of govern-
ment clients, and a wealth of talented employees. It was by far the
best professional option I had at that point in my life.

I traveled across the country to Washington for the interview,
and when my plane landed, my stomach started to hurt. I thought
it was just nerves or maybe the long flight, but when I got to my
hotel, my symptoms worsened. So I did what any genius in his
twenties would do. I lay in bed and watched a movie, hoping that
I would fall asleep and everything would be fine in the morning
when I had to get up and interview. Two movies later, I could
barely get out of bed. I slowly stood up and looked in the mirror.
Pale and doubled over in pain, I realized way later than I should

have that this was more than nerves. I limped out of the room and asked the front desk to call a taxi. The cab took me to the nearest hospital where a quick scan showed that I needed immediate surgery.

And that was the wonderful start to my interview experience.

Fortunately, my sister lived nearby and came to be with me at the hospital. She called the company and told them the situation while I lay on a gurney, sedated by a morphine drip. The company was more than gracious. They told me to take the time I needed to recover and that they would still interview me when I was ready.

After a week of recovering at my sister's house, I went to the office to interview. Believe it or not, I think my appendicitis worked in my favor. Everyone in the office knew the story when I arrived. They thought the timing and circumstance of getting appendicitis right before my interview was hilarious. "Sam, if you didn't want to interview, why didn't you just say so?" one employee said. It was a great icebreaker, although I still wouldn't recommend appendicitis as a means to warm up your interviewers. Not worth it.

The big interview that day was with Marty, a partner in the firm. He and I had spoken on the phone previously, so I wasn't going in blind. Plus, I wasn't writhing in pain anymore—always a bonus. But I did create a different kind of pain in the interview. It still makes me cringe when I think about it. One of the first questions Marty asked me was, "Why do you want this job?" Maybe it was the drugs. Maybe it was nerves. Maybe it was the folly of youth. Whatever it was, I'm embarrassed to admit that I said, "Actually, I'm not sure if I want this job. There is another job that I'm considering, and I'm having a tough time deciding between the two. And besides, I'm not even sure I want to live in the Washington, DC, area."

Note to self and to reader: if you are interviewing for a job, then, by definition, you don't yet have the job. It is therefore a bad idea to respond to questions as if you already have it. That's exactly what I did. I said I was having a tough time deciding when there was no decision yet to be made. Worse, I had put the interviewer in an awkward position. He had given me a shot at a great opportunity, flown me out to Washington, DC, put me up in a hotel, waited an extra week while I had surgery, and changed his schedule to interview me; was he now really supposed to convince me that I should be interested in this job?

On the flip side, I was being honest. And lying in an interview isn't good. But there are so many other things—great things—I could have said that also would have been honest. I could have talked about what I loved about the company after doing my research. I could have talked about why this position was a fantastic next step for me in my career. I could have talked about what a great new adventure it would be to live in Washington, DC! All these responses would have been honest too. All my internal turmoil (no pun intended) about my decision should have been saved for when I had been given the job offer in writing.

Marty was gracious. He helped me think through my different options, all the while smiling in a way that told me he was humoring me. Clearly, this was not something he was used to doing. When the interview ended, he told me he appreciated my candor, and I got an offer the next week.

But I really shouldn't have gotten this job. There is a piece of the story I haven't told you. My sister (the one who lived nearby) worked for the company. She was the reason I had gotten the interview in the first place because she had given me a warm introduction to Marty a few months earlier. Marty and I had had a phone conversation where he mentored and coached me on my career. I had sent him writing samples. We'd talked about college life. By the time we met in person for an interview, he was almost a friend. Had I given Marty my "I'm not sure I want this job" answer without having a previous relationship, I'm certain I would have been shown the door.

Side note: this story demonstrates, yet again, the tremendous advantage you can get in an interview if you take the time to leverage your contacts and conduct informational interviews. Because I had done that, the job was mine to lose from the moment I stepped into the interview.

The Power of Starting with Momentum

The question Marty asked me was a typical introductory question. These are questions asked at the beginning of the interview that can sound like "Tell me about yourself" or "Walk me through your résumé" or "Tell me why you are here" or, in Marty's case, "Why do you want this job?" Sometimes the question is a combination of multiple questions. "Why don't you walk me through your résumé and tell me how you got to this point and why you are looking to join our organization," for example.

Let me tell you what these questions mean. If they were asking the question in a way that described exactly what they wanted to hear, they would say, "Take me chronologically through the most important experiences on your résumé, highlighting the most impressive and relevant parts, doing it in a way that shows you have skills and experience that perfectly match this position. As you do this, drop a few hints that you are a top performer by highlighting a strong result once in a while or a promotion here and there. Then tell me why you chose to apply for this job in a way that seems undeniably logical and doesn't sound desperate. Then make me feel like my company is the best one on earth and that working for it would be a dream come true—again, in a way that doesn't sound desperate. And please do this in less than three minutes. If you go longer than that, I will tune out. Okay, thanks."

If they were more succinct, they would say, "Tell me why you are the perfect person for this job."

Please internalize how much interviewers want to hire candidates. They are likely slammed at work and desperate to find help. That's why they are hiring someone in the first place. If they could skip the interview process altogether and just find the right person, they'd probably pay money to do it. They deeply want you to be an amazing candidate, and they want you to tell them as much so they can hire you and get back to work.

Your opportunity to start telling them comes right at the beginning of the interview. Why wait? Your response to the first question is your chance to spoon-feed them exactly what they are looking for. If you do this well, you will create what all candidates wish for in a job interview: momentum. Interview momentum is an invisible but powerful force. You can feel it when it's there. It sets a positive tone for the rest of the interview, like riding a bike with the wind at your back. Everything feels a little less forced for both you and the interviewer. You are happy it's going well, and you are excited to take on more questions. Your interviewer is happy it's going well and feels excited to ask you more questions. All this comes because you successfully created momentum with your first answer.

In some extreme cases, the momentum you create in response to an introductory question can get you the job on the spot.

Remember in chapter 1, where I cited a study that said most people make up their minds after the first five minutes of the interview? Well, the same study said that 30 percent of people *do* make up their minds in the first five minutes. That's a huge percentage. In fact, it's not unheard of for an employer to say, "Great, you're hired; when can you start?" after a candidate has delivered a great response to their first question. Do you believe this is possible? It is. It could happen to you.

Persuade Without Being Pushy

Some interview coaches disagree with the approach of pitching oneself immediately. They believe that your answer to introductory questions should be mild; that it's just a warm-up that allows both parties to settle in and get to know one another before diving into the real questions. Too much selling right away, they say, will turn off a hiring manager.

Wrong. It will turn off the hiring manager only if the candidate approaches this question without tact. Don't get me wrong: you should be selling yourself in your first response, but you should do it in a way that doesn't look like you are selling yourself. You should be persuasive but not pushy.

This is a critical skill not only for your response to the introductory question but also for your whole interview and throughout your whole career. Every corporate position has an element of sales to it. Each employee should be driving their agenda and selling. Throughout my career, I've sat in hundreds of meetings where a difficult problem arose and spiraled into confusion and discord because no one could persuade tactfully. I've also sat in hundreds of meetings where a master persuader, dedicated to their craft, navigated the group to a solution. I believe it's an art form that everyone must learn to reach certain levels of career success.

As I've observed people who have mastered persuasion without pushiness, I've learned that everyone has their own unique approach. Everyone does it in their own style based on their personality. Yet, at the same time, there are some core principles that each persuader practices. They can be applied directly to the opening statement of your job interview. Here they are.

Express gratitude: It's difficult to think someone is pushy when they are thanking you. Persuaders know this. A quick "Thank you for taking the time to interview me, I really appreciate it" with a smile starts an interview off in a positive way that makes the hiring manager feel good.

Use facts instead of claims: "Trust me" is not a believable claim at work, nor is it believable in your job interview. One of the ironies of trust is that telling people to trust you makes them trust you less. Instead, you should give people reasons to believe that you are a rock star and let them make up their minds themselves. Instead of telling them that you are a collaborative leader, an analytical wiz, or great at social media, show them. Use numbers or stories. Both can be incorporated as you answer introductory questions.

Respect a person's right not to believe you: The most persuasive pitches I've seen are those that respect the audience's right not to be persuaded. When people don't feel pressured into being persuaded, they are more open to it. There is no need to be skeptical when they know that you are perfectly fine with them disagreeing with you.

Radiate positivity: Negativity can be a good persuasive tool in some contexts (politics, anyone?) but not in a job interview. Being negative about a prior job or boss can derail your opening statement quickly. Now, instead of focusing on your great experience and fitness for the role, the interviewer is worried about whether you have an attitude problem. You are allowed to have negative experiences at work, of course, but you aren't allowed to dump that onto your interviewer (unless, of course, you don't want the job). In my personal hiring, I've turned a candidate down solely because they spoke negatively about their prior job. They may have been a talented candidate, but someone who comes into an interview with a negative attitude poses too much risk for my preference. Persuasive job candidates are optimists.

Develop Your Opening Statement

Let's walk through how you should respond to an introductory question. Remember, there are many ways they can ask an introductory question, but they all want you to respond as if they are asking, "Why are you the perfect person for this job?" So you need to develop only one response that tells them you are their dream come true. I call this your opening statement. A good opening statement highlights three things to the interviewer: First, that you have the right skills for the job. Second, that you are a top performer. Third, that you are very interested in the position.

Let's look at how to craft each of the three.

Skills: After you thank them for the opportunity to interview and express how much you are looking forward to the conversation, start walking them through your prior experience in a structured way. I have found that it's easiest for interviewers to follow along if you structure your experiences chronologically, as they are listed on your résumé. I prefer to start with my experiences right out of college and work my way to the present time, but you may prefer to do it in reverse. Just make sure it's structured and easy to follow.

What if you are just coming out of college and don't have a long list of work experiences to draw from? No problem. Highlight any part-time work you've done or internships you've held. It's great to highlight projects you've done in school classes. All of this is fine as long as you keep it relevant to the job description.

As you go through each experience, highlight in simple terms what the company did and what your responsibilities were that pertain to the job. You don't need to give a lot of context, and you don't need to focus on all your responsibilities. Probably the biggest temptation you'll have in answering introductory questions is to mention skills and experiences the employer isn't looking for. Resist the urge to tell them everything on your mind or all experiences you've had. Just because you've worked hard at something doesn't mean the interviewer cares about it. You should focus only on things the employer cares about. For example, if the new role is highly analytical, highlight the analytical parts of your past experiences. If analytics has nothing to do with the role, then don't mention it and focus on more pertinent experiences.

Results: As you walk through your experiences, briefly summarizing what the company did and your scope of responsibilities, work in results that you've achieved. Highlighting results tells the interviewer that you have a track record of excellence. This could come in the form of mentioning that you were quickly promoted, that you were given more responsibility than your peers, that you had a big impact on a prior business in the short time you were there, or that you won an award as best marketer of the year or top salesperson for the month. You don't have to be lengthy, and you don't have to do it for every experience you mention, but you should leave no doubt in your opening statement that you are a performer.

Use the worksheet below to help you structure how you talk about your experiences.

Target Role:
Social Media Marketing for an Outdoor Gear Company

Experience 1: marketing internship while in college
Company: Protein Shakes Inc., a twenty-employee company that sold protein shake powder to natural food stores
Relevant scope of responsibility: Learned to manage Instagram and Facebook (which are the primary platforms used by this outdoor gear company)
Compelling result: Grew their platform followers by ten times
Experience 2: social media manager
Company: Get Social, a social media agency that specializes in helping clients grow their social media presence
Relevant scope of responsibility: Managed social media platforms and tracked return on ad spend (ROAS). (Analyzing ROAS is a critical part of this job.)
Compelling result: Was quickly promoted to manager after increasing our biggest client's ROAS from 1.5 to 2 in six months.
Experience 3: e-commerce manager
Company: Furniturefun.com, an online retailer that focuses on selling aftermarket furniture
Relevant scope of responsibility: Managed social media platforms and tracked return on ad spend (ROAS). (Analyzing ROAS is a critical part of this job.)
Compelling result: Identified as a top performer and was given additional furniture categories to manage after my first year of being there

Interest: Skills and results are only the first part of your answer. They convince them that you are a great fit for the role. Now you need to convince them that the role is a great fit for you. Why do they care that you get something out of it besides money? Because they want to believe that you will accept the job if it's offered to you and maybe even stay a while. They want to believe that you will learn and grow and find fulfillment. They know that you won't be around long if it's not a great fit for you, so you need to persuade them that this will be a mutually beneficial relationship.

But how? By pointing out something the job offers that you want. A particular culture, a new skill set, new responsibility, the ability to expand your impact. As long as it is genuine and thoughtful, it will have an impact.

Opening Statement Examples

Example One: You are applying for a job as a social media manager for Walmart. You have about five years of postgraduate experience. You start the interview and the first question the interviewer asks is, "Can you walk me through your résumé and tell me why you are here?"

Answer: Yes! Thank you so much for taking the time to interview me. I'm really excited about this opportunity. I graduated from the University of Wisconsin five years ago in business management with an emphasis on marketing. During my schooling, I managed the social media accounts for the university bookstore, and that's where I decided that I really liked digital marketing.

Right after my experience in business management, I went to work for MediaWorks, a local digital marketing agency in Wisconsin, where I managed several clients' digital marketing efforts. Among my clients were local auto dealerships, grocery stores, and some clothing stores.

After two years at MediaWorks, I left to go to the client side and worked for a large clothing chain, Cool Threads, and managed their digital efforts as well. I've been there three years and have had a really good experience.

Now I'm applying for this position with Walmart because it's the biggest retailer in the world, and I would love the opportunity to leverage the skills that I have learned on a bigger scale, while also learning more about the retail side of things.

How was that? Not bad. In fact, pretty good, right? But it wasn't great.

Why not? First, I didn't explain my experience enough for the interviewer to know exactly what I did. For example, instead of just saying, "I managed digital marketing," I could have said, "I managed their digital marketing and was responsible for growing their audience on Facebook. And during those two years, I became a Facebook expert, gaining a full understanding of the Facebook ad platform."

Second, I didn't go into the results that I achieved with each of my experiences. For example, when I talked about managing the social media for the university bookstore, I could have said something like, "I managed the social media accounts for the university bookstore. During that time, I grew our followers by 200 percent. I was able to do this by figuring out the right type of content that worked for our audience as well as engaging with other university influencers."

And third, while I expressed interest in the role, I could have done a much better job explaining why my experiences were perfect for the role and why I was so interested. For example, I could have said, "One of the accounts that I loved managing was the local grocery store chain. In fact, I even persuaded my client to let me shadow her for a day so that I could learn a bit more about it. I knew I wanted to get into the retail side of things, so I did a lot of research on where I should go and ultimately landed on Walmart. I am interested in Walmart because Walmart is really forward thinking when it comes to retail marketing. I've been monitoring the company's social media content strategy for a while now, and I really appreciate how much it's shifted toward social media to notify consumers of your price promotions. I've also spoken with a few people in the department and have walked away with a pretty good sense of the culture. And I think the collaborative way Walmart works is a good fit for me."

By saying those things, you've indicated exactly why you want to get into retail and exactly why you want to work for Walmart. You have demonstrated that you did your homework and you basically told them that if this job were offered to you, you would take it!

Example Two: This time, suppose that I am about to graduate from college and I'm applying for a job as a sales rep for Samsung.

Thank you for taking the time to interview me. Let me take you through my résumé and talk about why I am interested in working in the technology industry and, specifically,

Samsung. Growing up, I was always fascinated by and interested in technology. I took every opportunity in high school to be around it. I found that, while I was good at working with technology, I was actually better at explaining to others how it works. In fact, when I was in high school, I was paid several times to help set up phones and apps for my friends' parents as well as training them in how to use them.

When I started college, I needed a way to pay the bills, so I took a job with Best Buy as a sales representative on the floor. This allowed me to use my knack for explaining technology, and it also taught me a lot more about products. I became very familiar with Samsung's full lineup of phones and TVs and learned how to sell them to others. In fact, I wound up being the top salesperson in my store in my second year, and I have stayed in the top 10 percent of salespeople since then.

I chose to major in marketing and sales so that I could hone my ability to work with people and sell. I joined the sales club at my university and persuaded the club to put more emphasis on technology sales. I even formed a group that met bimonthly to discuss sales careers in the technology industry.

During my work at Best Buy and in my coursework, I learned a lot about Samsung products and gained a passion for them. I really believe many of the products are superior to the competition, especially the TV lines. I believe I could be a great ambassador for Samsung as a salesperson. I understand each product's advantages and have been successful at selling them for three years now. I am genuinely interested in working for Samsung and I've really been looking forward to this interview!

This is an A-plus response. Let's look at the three things I accomplished:

First, I clearly laid out my experiences. And, since I was just graduating from college, I even went back to some things I did in high school, which is totally cool as long as it's relevant. The interviewer was left with no doubt about what I did. I set up Samsung products for people in their homes, and then I sold Samsung products at Best Buy. Check. Oh, and I didn't just say I worked at Best Buy. I said I was a sales representative on the floor. People know exactly what this is.

Then I demonstrated strong results with each experience I shared. I told them I was so good at technology as a kid that I created a business around it, helping my friends' parents. I said I was a top salesperson at Best Buy, and in college I created a group to discuss sales careers in the technology industry. Even though not all of these were quantifiable, the initiative I showed will be interpreted as results, demonstrating that I am someone who makes things happen.

Finally, I explained why this would be a good fit by working in to my stories that I was naturally good with technology products and that I was passionate about Samsung products.

Now, after looking at these examples, you may be thinking, "Great, Sam, but my experience doesn't line up this nicely for the job I want." Maybe you are trying to switch careers. Perhaps you have a degree in Russian literature and are now trying to get a job doing something other than teaching Russian literature.

If you have experience that doesn't feel like a slam dunk for the job description, you can identify more general, translatable skills that you have. For example, the friend I mentioned in chapter 3 who studied history in school but landed a job with Disney in marketing. He pulled it off by showing that his interest in history was centered on an interest in human behavior, which is ultimately at the core of marketing. There is almost always a way to find a bridge from what you have done to what you are trying to do. If there isn't even a hint of a bridge, maybe it's not the right job for you or maybe you need to go back to school to create a more compelling story.

You've now nailed the answer to your first question—well done! Now you have positive mojo going into the next section of the interview. You're going to need it because you're now likely to face your next challenge: behavioral questions.

Chapter Summary

Starting the interview off strong means reframing "Tell me about yourself" to "Tell me about why you are the perfect fit for this job?"

Answer the first question by persuading without being pushy; express gratitude, use facts instead of claims, respect a person's right to disagree, radiate positivity.

Your opening statement should convey that you have three things:

- Skills: the experiences you walk them through should be easy to understand and related to the job description.
- Results: highlight a positive result you achieved in each experience—business results, promotions, and an

increase in responsibility all can pass as results at this stage.

- Interest: give unique reasons for why you are so interested in this company and role.

Preparation Checklist Progress

Opening statement	
Does it demonstrate that you are qualified?	✔
Does it show that you get results?	✔
Does it show that you are genuinely interested in the job?	✔

six.
tell compelling stories

Mastering Behavioral Questions

When the COVID-19 pandemic hit in March 2020, I wasn't very concerned. Sure, I was aware of the situation and understood the facts. I knew that it had started in China and was making its way across the world. I understood that it was highly contagious and that it affected the elderly more than the general population. I recognized that it could kill millions—even tens of millions—of people.

Yet even knowing these facts, I wasn't all that worried. As calloused as it sounds, I categorized the pandemic with other big global challenges I saw on the news, such as natural disasters or global hunger. These problems, while terrible, did not have a major impact on my daily life. As a result, I could describe them with facts and figures but keep them at arm's length. That's exactly how I viewed the pandemic.

Then my mom's cousin contracted COVID on a trip to Palm Springs while visiting friends. He started feeling sick when he returned to his home in Los Angeles. Before long, he was admitted to a hospital and put on a respirator. As our extended family anxiously awaited his status, I learned more about this cousin. I discovered that he had had a successful career in finance in New York City and was a dedicated community servant and member of his church. I learned that he had built a great family, with children and grandchildren who loved him. My family tracked his progress until he died alone at the hospital. Tragically, because of COVID restrictions, his kids could not be with him in his final hours to say goodbye.

His story changed everything for me. For the first time, COVID became deeply personal. I felt terrible for his family and concerned for my own. I wanted to protect my parents from getting the virus. I felt terrible for all who had gotten or who would get it. It brought the pandemic to life in a way that had a bigger effect on me than all the COVID facts and figures combined.

Our brains are wired for stories. When we hear a good story, we learn something new, but more important, we feel emotion. A story that inspires emotion solidifies the information in our minds and makes it memorable. It also motivates us to change our behavior. Good stories can persuade someone to start obeying the speed limit or donate to a charitable cause or hire someone after a job interview.

You should use stories more than data in a job interview. Data are forgettable, stories are memorable. Data are general, stories are specific. Data are complex, stories are simple. Data are standoffish and cold, stories are relatable and warm. Data are debatable, stories are irrefutable. Data bore, stories motivate. Data raise questions, stories put things to rest. In a job interview, if you talk only about data without using stories, you'll not only fail to answer the questions fully, but you'll bore your interviewer to tears.

Stories are also better than principles and platitudes. A principle provides no evidence of your ability. An interviewer may agree with you about a principle related to the job but still be left wondering if you have the skills to do the work. Only by providing a specific, factual, engaging example will you prove that you have the skills they are looking for.

In this chapter, you'll learn how to tell concise, relevant, and engaging stories in a job interview. I'll first teach you how to recognize a question that calls for a story. Then I'll take you through a step-by-step storytelling model that works every time. As you learn and practice the models, you'll demonstrate that you have the skills for the job and create an advantage for yourself in the interview.

Show, Don't Tell

Aron Ralston is a mountaineer who cut off his own arm to save his life. I asked him to speak at my company in 2015. I worked for a $4 billion food corporation and was responsible for finding someone to talk to the marketing department about grit and determination. Historically, when we selected speakers for an event at my company, we met beforehand to "brief" them. We'd tell them why we wanted them to speak and what specific things we wanted them to cover. We sometimes would warn them about sensitive topics in the organization and tell them what not to say. This process allowed us to control the narrative and make sure we were getting what we wanted. But our conversation with Aron was different. "Just tell your story," we said.

Aron showed up to the event in a suit. We shook (left) hands, and he jumped on stage. For the next hour, he told us in detail of his five days trapped in a slot canyon with his hand under a rock. He described his efforts to break free using everything he had learned as an engineer and mountaineer. He told us about drinking his own urine to stay hydrated. Finally, he described in painful detail his inevitable decision to break his arm with his own weight, then sever it with a dull knife. This group of rambunctious marketers was utterly silent for sixty minutes. The only exceptions were those who had to step out during the graphic parts because they couldn't take it, and those who teared up when he told about his mother being inside the helicopter that rescued him.

Aron could have filled his speech with principles on grit and determination. He could have given us a list of his beliefs on the subject and some ideas on how we could apply them in our own lives. But none of it could have compared to the grit and determination demonstrated through his story. Aron didn't tell us; he showed us.

Showing, not telling, is the first rule in telling great stories in job interviews, and you do it by being specific. Far too many candidates spew out chunks of separate stories or, worse, talk only in generalities. They start with, "I always try to," or "I believe in," or "I think it's important to," and then go on to highlight principles that anyone would agree with but that don't demonstrate their abilities. Only when you provide a specific story will you clearly show that you have the skills to do the job.

Let me illustrate with a scenario that doesn't involve cutting off your arm. Imagine interviewing Realtors to decide which one you'd like to hire to sell your house. You want to know how good they are at preparing a house to look "show ready." You might ask, "How good are you at preparing houses to sell?" To this, the Realtor could respond, "I am exceptionally good at it. I always make every house looks top notch" or "I'm the best in my field. Trust me." This sounds great. You want it to be true, but you have no evidence. You then decide to be more specific and ask, "What is your approach to getting a house ready?" This response will help you a little more. It will give you some detail, but you will still likely get some general thoughts as a response, and you'll still have no proof that the Realtor follows this approach in practice. Now, you wise up and say, "Tell me about the last home you sold. What was your specific approach to preparing the home for sale, and what happened as a result?" Now the Realtor must explain in concrete terms how she used her skills to successfully prepare a home for sale. You'll learn about her approach, and you'll have evidence (or not) for her claims.

This is why behavioral questions are common. Interviewers believe that if you can show them that you've demonstrated a skill in the past, you'll likely demonstrate that skill in the future. Behavioral questions are asked in most corporate job interviews. You know they are asking you a behavioral question when they start with "Tell me about a time when," "Can you give me an example in your past experience of," or "Please share how you have." By asking a question this way, they invite you to tell a specific story in a specific way. They will also ask a more general question like, "What is your leadership style" or "How do you work with others." Even though these questions don't directly ask for a story, a story often is the best way to answer the question.

I'm going to teach you exactly how to tell these stories the way interviewers want to hear them so that you can quickly and concisely demonstrate that you have the skills for the job.

Bucket Your Stories by Skill

Want to give yourself a panic attack? As you prepare for your interview, write down every possible behavioral question that you might be asked and formulate a great story for each one. How do you think that will work out? You will quickly find yourself very heavy on questions and very light on stories. You'll realize there are hundreds—even thousands—of behavioral questions that they could ask you. You don't have enough stories in your experience to answer them all. If you do, they probably aren't all winners.

Let's try a less stressful, more effective approach. Instead of guessing which questions you might be asked, focus on which skills they are looking for. A short list of skills can be found by reading the job description, researching the company online, and speaking with people who have worked for the company.

Suppose your research reveals that they want someone who can lead others, has analytical ability, can think strategically, works well with others, and has a drive for results. Now you're getting somewhere! You have just taken hundreds of potential questions and bucketed them into a manageable list of question *categories*. Here are some examples of how this works:

Skill: leadership
Potential questions: Tell me about a time when you . . .

. . . led a team through a difficult business challenge.

. . . led a team to accomplish an important objective.

. . . went against the consensus for an initiative in which you deeply believed.

... had to make a tough decision you felt was the right thing to do.

... had to motivate a team that had previously been unmotivated.

Skill: analytical ability
Potential questions: Tell me about a time when you . . .

... managed a complex project.

... used your critical thinking skills to solve a business problem.

... took something complicated and made it simple.

... used your brain to think through a problem involving numbers.

... used numbers to persuade someone on your team.

Skill: strategic thinking
Potential questions: Tell me about a time when you . . .

... created a business strategy for a business that was declining.

... conducted an assessment of a business model.

... thought through how your product was different from that of a competitor.

... put together a cohesive action plan for your boss.

Skill: working well with others

Potential questions: Tell me about a time when you . . .

. . . had a difficult boss or coworker and still had to develop a strong working relationship.

. . . had a challenging person on your team that hindered your team's progress.

. . . had to persuade someone to your way of thinking.

. . . had to admit that you were wrong.

Skill: drive for results

Potential questions: Tell me about a time when you . . .

. . . exceeded the expectations placed on you.

. . . missed a critical business objective. How did you react?

. . . went above and beyond what was asked of you because you wanted to reach a goal.

. . . motivated other people toward achieving a goal.

See what I mean? The list of questions is long, but the number of skills assessed is small. For example, suppose a company is looking for leadership skills. In that case, the recruiter may ask, "Tell me about a time when you had to lead a team," "Tell me about a time when you had to make a difficult decision that affected other employees," or "Tell me about a time when you had someone who worked for you who had lost motivation to work hard." A trained ear can immediately recognize these questions as interpersonal leadership questions. Just because there may be twenty different ways of asking a leadership question doesn't mean you must develop twenty different responses. You only need one or two strong examples of interpersonal leadership, and then you can position your answers slightly differently, depending on the exact question you are asked.

Use the SPAR Model

I took my family to Disneyland for the third time a few years ago. We had a magical time, but my behavior on the trip went against my better financial judgment. Disney tickets are well over $100 per day. The food prices are through the roof. The lines are horrific. And despite there being an amusement park close to my house in Denver, I was happy to pay for plane tickets and a hotel in Southern California so that we could be at Disneyland.

I'm not alone in my insanity. Parents all over the world prioritize Disney over other amusement parks, even though it's well more than double the price. Why do they pay this premium? Stories. The Walt Disney Company has been telling captivating stories for nearly a century, and they bring those stories to life at their theme parks. As Disney former executive vice president Andrew Sugerman said, "Storytelling is literally in our DNA." With $68 billion in annual revenue, I think their DNA just might be on to something.

We can learn a lot from a Disney movie as it relates to job interviewing. Pick any Disney movie, from *The Lion King* to *Toy Story* to *The Avengers*, and you'll notice a formula like this:

- *Situation:* The hero lives in a world with certain rules and norms.

- *Problem:* The hero encounters a dramatic problem that must be solved.
- *Action:* The hero works most of the movie to solve the problem.
- *Result:* The hero solves the problem, and everything works out great in the end.

Disney movies follow the SPAR format. They set up a clear situation, they have a problem that creates drama, they have a hero who takes action to solve the problem, and everything works out fabulously well in the end.

Of course, job interview stories are different from Disney movies. In a job interview, for example, you should tell your story in about three to five minutes, not two hours. If you take less than three minutes, the interviewer's question isn't fully answered. If you take more than five minutes, you are almost certainly rambling. But the core idea is the same. Great stories follow the SPAR format, and they do it in that order. Just knowing the SPAR model, however, is not enough. You must understand how much time to spend on each area and which parts of the story matter the most. I'll take you through each part of the model and show you how to put it together with some examples.

Set up a specific situation.

When you start your story, give a brief setup so they can understand the context for the key points you'll make later. The key to a good setup is brevity. The situation part of your answer is important, but it isn't the part people want to hear. You only need to give the backstory that is relevant to your story. If you are asked a question about analytical ability, does the size of the company you worked for or the fact that you had a challenging boss matter?

We're talking one to three sentences here. If you are going over thirty seconds with backstory, it's too long. Here are some good examples of setups:

> "Last year, I was working as an operations manager for a food manufacturing plant, and I was responsible for making sure their three biggest production lines ran efficiently."

> "For the last three years, I have been working as an investment manager for a Bank of America retail location. My job is to help clients with their investment portfolio and to sell them new financial products."

> "I recently worked as a content writer for a social media ad agency. My job was to create and post several pieces of content per day for our biggest client."

> "Two years ago, I worked as a project manager, handling our top five biggest clients. I was responsible for ensuring that their IT needs were always met and that we delivered on time and on budget."

Highlight a problem.

Just like in a Disney movie, this is where the story gets interesting. The problem creates drama and intrigue. Interviewers are known to get quite bored during an interview, especially if they do many interviews in one day. A little tension will keep them interested! It makes them want to listen to find out how the problem will be solved.

For example, if you are asked about a time when you had to manage a difficult coworker, you could say, "One of my coworkers was a challenge." That would be factual, but it does nothing to create real tension or spark curiosity. But if you said, "One of my peers had been at the organization a lot longer than I had, and she clearly wasn't interested in helping me be successful. In the first three months, she would leave me out of meetings and not give me the correct information I needed. I think she saw me as a threat, but I knew that, to be successful, we needed to have a strong working relationship," you have now grabbed the interviewer's attention. She will want to keep listening to see how you solved this problem.

Granted, it is relatively easy to create tension with people problems. But what about a more boring topic, like analytics? For example, you could say, "I was asked to create a system for tracking all inventory of our baby clothes." You could stop there if you want to bore the interviewer. Why not add a little drama and create some tension? Consider adding, "Two previous attempts at tracking that inventory had failed." Or you could say, "We were losing $2 million a year in wasted inventory at the time, and this was a top priority at the company."

Walk them through your actions.

This is the meat of your answer and where you should spend most of your time. Most of a Disney story is about the hero's actions to solve a problem because that is where the hero learns, grows, and demonstrates their ability. It's the same in a job interview. Your interviewer cares most about your ability.

A great way to answer this question is to use the "rule of three," which means you list three separate actions that you took to solve the problem. Doing it this way provides structure and simplicity to your answer so that the interviewer can easily follow along. In fact, the interviewer is often taking notes. They may even have some version of the SPAR method already written down, and they are just looking for you to spoon-feed them the correct answers so they can fill in the blanks. Then they will take their notes to other decision-makers and read exactly what you spoon-fed them. Of course, it doesn't have to be exactly three things, but it should have a sequence and a structure.

This action portion is no time to be modest. This is about what *you* did. Not your team, not you together with your coworker. Take credit for your great work. If you can't find anything in your story to take credit for, find another story.

Let's go back to the difficult coworker example. You could say, "The first thing I realized was that I needed to build a relationship with that person, so I first took her to lunch and got to know her personally. I listened to her carefully and realized we had a lot in common. I learned that she went to high school in a neighboring town and we knew some of the same people. I learned about the pressures she was facing at work and how her boss was giving her more and more difficult assignments. Just listening to her experiences helped us connect personally. The second thing I did was set up biweekly meetings with her. Then I asked her if she would be my informal mentor on the company culture. I told her I needed to learn and that she had a lot to teach me. She agreed, and we started a great mentoring relationship where she helped me better understand the company and its history. Finally, as time went on, I found an opportunity to help her with a difficult assignment. She was responsible for reducing downtime on our manufacturing lines, and I had learned a little about that in a previous job. I gave her some suggestions, she implemented them, and the results made her look great in front of her boss."

After listing the three things you did, you could summarize the key principles for the interviewer. For example, you could say, "Overcoming this challenge was really about building a personal relationship, reaching out and having her be my mentor, and helping her be successful."

Offer a compelling result.

No Disney movie is complete without a happy ending, and no job interview is complete unless it ends with a compelling result. It's time to tie your story in a bow for the interviewer by giving a brief statement that shows everything worked out just fine and your actions delivered the desired result.

Try to quantify your results wherever possible. That is easier to do with some questions, such as analytical questions. For example, "As a result of building my inventory management system, we saved $300,000 during the next year." Other questions feel harder to quantify, such as interpersonal leadership questions. But even with more subjective questions, you can come up with a great, tangible result. For example, "As a result, we became very close friends, and this person's performance has increased over the last three quarters." This is a great response because, while it's a subjective topic, you are still pointing to some objective, fact-based results.

Push yourself to come up with a great result. If you don't, your story will be incomplete, and your interviewer will be left hanging.

Putting It All Together

I'm going to walk you through three examples. These may not be the exact questions you'll be asked in your next job interview, but they will demonstrate how the SPAR model works so that you can create your own stories. They are great templates to use as you develop your personal stories.

Example one

Question: Can you tell me about a time when you had to persuade others to your way of thinking on a business decision? (This is a working-well-with-others question. They are trying to see how you go about persuading other people.)

> *Situation:* Last summer, I was a marketing intern for a clothing retailer. My project was to work with our website team to refresh our website design to boost our online sales.

> *Problem:* Halfway through the summer, I realized that this project had a lot of opposition from our in-store merchandising group. They felt that, if online sales were boosted, it would take away from their in-store sales. This was a real challenge because the in-store sales group created most of the company's revenue and thus carried a lot of weight, so it was up to this lowly intern to make a case for online sales while at the same time making sure the in-store group felt good about it.

> *Action:* To address the problem, I did three things.

1. I found out who the key players were in this in-store merchandising group and set up mentoring lunches with them. That move allowed me to not only get to know them personally but, most important, to listen to what their concerns were so that (a) they knew I was listening and (b) I could work to address them.

2. It turned out that the biggest concern really was, as you would expect, top-line sales being taken away from their stores. I did a lot of research on other companies with a strong online presence and found out that the overlap between in-store selling and online sales was not very high. And, in fact, I saw that, with many retailers, sometimes the online presence actually drove people into the store because they wanted to try the clothes on themselves. I compiled all this external data to prepare for my final presentation. Then I put together a recommendation to test this idea in a couple of regions before rolling it out nationally. That way, we could prove that online did, in fact, help in-store performance.

3. Finally, I made a special effort to show my presentation to the online retail group before my final presentation to the company executives. This allowed me to hear all their concerns and talk about those concerns in my final presentation. They didn't agree with everything I said, but they felt I made an effort to listen and was ready to address those concerns if they came up in my final presentation.

Result: As a result of this, I was able to make a compelling presentation to the company executives that addressed the concerns of the in-store group. In the actual presentation, one of the in-store employees spoke up and said that, while they didn't agree with everything, I was one of the most collaborative interns they ever worked with.

So it was really about (1) building a personal relationship with and listening to those who oppose you; (2) letting the data and information do a lot of the persuading; and (3) then doing what you can to create an environment to let the facts win, like with this test I was recommending.

This is an excellent answer. I gave a clear setup of the situation in just two sentences. I created tension in the problem section by highlighting opposition and explaining how challenging it was for an intern to persuade a very powerful group. In my action section, I used the "rule of three." I discussed three things I did to improve the situation: setting up a personal relationship, gathering a lot of facts, and showing this group my presentation to build trust before I showed it to the corporate executives. Finally, I delivered fact-based results that were irrefutable.

Example two

Question: Can you tell me about a time when you had to think strategically? (Don't be thrown off by the word "strategy." This is just to test your ability to assess a business problem and come up with solutions.)

Situation: Two years ago, I was a college senior involved in student government. Specifically, I was responsible for getting donations from our alumni.

Problem: The challenge was that our donations had been down significantly for over a year because of the economy. And, over the previous six months, no one had been successful just making phone calls to get more donations. It just wasn't working.

Action: I approached this problem in three steps.

1. The first step was the research phase. I looked at all the donations from the previous year, where they came from, whether they came by mail or online or by phone, who the donors were, and what the donation amounts were. Given that information, I discerned that 80 percent of our donation dollars were coming from only 20 percent of those donating. Those donors were typically wealthy and usually contributed each year when asked. You could count on them. I also discovered that only 10 percent of our alumni were contributing. I did some additional research to find out that the most significant reason they didn't contribute was that they felt they had to contribute $50 or more since that's what they were usually asked to do. I could see from this information that our biggest upside was the 90 percent of alumni who didn't contribute.

2. I then developed a strategy for going after that 90 percent. Instead of asking them to contribute $50 or more, I created a plan to ask them for a lower amount. I projected that if we could get even a small percentage of those people to contribute, we could really grow.

3. And finally, I executed this plan by rolling it out to other volunteers. We created new scripts for our phone

calls and changed our mailers to reflect a new campaign called "$10 Matters."

Result: As a result of this effort, we grew our donations by 10 percent and exceeded all expectations for that year. In fact, to this day, I don't think they've surpassed what we did a couple of years ago.

This is another excellent example. I briefly set up the situation, showed that the problem was growing donations, did the research to figure out how I was going to solve that problem, and then created three steps to accomplish it.

Example three

Question: Can you tell me about a time when you had to solve a complex problem? (This is an analytical ability question.)

Situation: Most recently, I was an account manager for a digital marketing agency. I was responsible for a broad portfolio of client relationships and managing those relationships.

Problem: A few months into the job, I was asked to evaluate all our clients to determine which clients were most valuable to our company. This was a real challenge because it had never been done before, and there were no clear guidelines on how value was defined.

Action:

1. The first thing I did to understand the value of our clients was to create a scorecard of various measures to define that value. The first measure was top-line

revenue, the second was bottom-line profitability, and the third was a credibility score, based on how well-known that client was and how much it helped us get other clients.

2. Next, I layered on a measure of how many hours per month we spent on each client and divided those key three metrics by the hours to determine the ratio of how valuable the client was per hour. I did all of this with an Excel file.

3. Finally, I created a presentation for our executives after crunching the numbers. Some of our findings were surprising. For example, we often found that we were spending way too much time with certain clients that we weren't making any money on, even though they were providing a lot of publicity for our firm. And it also showed that we had a lot of upside to grow our business by putting in a little extra work with other clients.

Result: As a result of this analysis, we shifted our strategy to focus on a couple of extra-high-impact clients. Because of that extra focus, six months later, we were able to grow the revenue from those customers by 25 percent, a major contribution to the growth of the firm that year. As far as I know, that model is still in use today.

Another great example. I walked step-by-step through the way I solved the problem, but I kept the story simple enough not to lose the interviewer. Analytical questions can be tricky. They want to know whether you can break down problems and think them through structurally. You can't answer this so lightly that they don't understand your thinking, but you also can't get so deep into the weeds that they can't follow you. You must practice these answers in a very structured, "rule-of-three" way so they can follow what you did without getting confused.

Chapter Summary

Behavioral questions ask you to tell stories because stories are better than data, principles, or platitudes.

Show, don't tell, by creating specific stories demonstrating your skills to do the job.

Create five to seven power stories based on the skills the employer wants. Don't try to create a unique story for every possible behavioral question.

When telling stories, use the SPAR model:

- Situation: make it brief and related to the story.
- Problem: create tension, so the interviewer wants to keep listening.
- Action: explain what you uniquely did to solve the problem by using the "rule of three."
- Result: tie it in a bow.

Preparation Checklist Progress

5–7 behavioral responses (SPAR Model)	
Is there a quick setup?	✔
Is there tension and drama?	✔
Do you walk through your actions sequentially?	✔

seven.

use simple frameworks

Nailing Scenario Questions

I desperately wanted to intern for Nestlé when I was in business school. It was, and still is, the biggest food company in the world, and they offer their employees world-class training in marketing. After months of networking during my first year in my program, I finally got an opportunity to do a phone interview for a marketing intern position in their Glendale, California, office. I was ecstatic. I researched the company online and started conducting informational interviews. I spoke to people who worked for the company, some of whom had graduated from my school just a year or two before me and gave me great advice. Based on my initial research and preparation, I felt that I had a great shot at getting the internship. I also knew that if I did well in that role, I could pretty much pick any marketing job I wanted coming out of business school.

Interview day came. I went into a private room at my business school to take the call. Everything started out great. The interviewer and I seemed to hit it off fine. I came with energy and enthusiasm, and she matched it. It was encouraging. I nailed the introductory question, giving clear reasons why I was qualified and interested. I handled the behavioral questions equally well, telling compelling SPAR stories that provided strong evidence that I could do the job. Thirty minutes into the interview, I felt like things couldn't have been going better.

Then the hammer dropped. She went in for the kill by asking me a scenario question. "Sam, pick one of our brands," she asked. "Um, okay. I'll pick Butterfinger," I said. "Great! Congratulations, you are now the new brand manager for Butterfinger. You get into the office today and see a report that shows your business is down 10 percent this month versus last year. What things would you look at to figure out what's driving these losses?

It was a full mic drop for her, followed by a lot of rambling from me. I was caught flat-footed and went on a three-minute, incoherent tangent. I rattled off the first thing that came to my head, and then the next thing, and then the next thing. First, I mentioned that I should look at pricing, then I was afraid that I wouldn't think of anything else, so when "product" popped into my head, I immediately switched gears and started talking about that. Then, I thought of promotion. *Oh yes, promotion!* I thought. *That's important too.* I quickly jumped from product to promotion and started spewing out anything I could think of that I was taught in a recent marketing class. None of this came out smoothly or confidently. After I finished, I knew I had botched it. But I hoped that my prior responses would be good enough to still get me the offer. I thought that maybe I would get some forgiveness since, after all, I was just a first-year MBA student, and this was just an internship.

But no such forgiveness came. I don't remember whether she gave me feedback right after that question or if she waited until the end of the interview. Either way, before we got off the phone, she told me in no uncertain terms that I would not be moving on to the next step in the interview process. I had failed the interview.

I've had some bad interview experiences, but this one stands out as particularly painful. The stakes were so high for me in that phase of my life. I needed a great internship. I had a wife and son, not to mention a daughter on the way. I had quit my job to go back to school, and we were making ends meet only through government assistance. The pressure was intense. I knew that the better the internship I secured that summer, the stronger the position I would be in upon graduation. I had just failed the most important interview of my life up to that point. With the little experience of the business world I had at the time, I felt like this single event would be a missed opportunity that I would feel for the rest of my career.

That wasn't true, of course. I bounced back and found a great job. It's a distant, albeit still slightly painful, memory. I think the real reason it stung so badly is that I knew I could have gotten that internship. Many of my peers in school were getting internships just like this one and succeeding in them. It was not a situation where I lacked the talent or qualifications. I had simply underestimated how much preparation would be required to nail a scenario question.

The Hardest Questions of Them All

Scenario interview questions, also known as hypothetical, situational, or case questions, are open-ended questions that require you to formulate answers in real time, based on a real-world scenario.

They sound like this:

- How would you approach your first ninety days on this job?
- What areas of opportunity do you see for our business?
- How would go about making an upset customer happy?
- How would you compete against our business if you were our competitor?
- Which of our competitors is doing the best job in the market and why?
- If you were offered this position, how would you go about building relationships with key players in this office?
- What would your approach be for building our social media presence?
- Tell me what you think about this piece of advertising. How would you make it better?
- What would you do if you were given an assignment with an unreasonable timeline?

For most candidates, scenario questions are the most challenging questions in the entire interview, and for good reason. First, there are no right or wrong answers, even though they are structured to sound like there are. When someone asks, "How many gas stations are there in San Francisco?" the average candidate believes the interviewer has an exact number in mind. The same is true even with a nonnumerical question like "Which of our competitors do you think are doing really well right now and why?" All your schooling has trained you to believe that there is a "correct" answer to this question.

Second, the interviewer has an information advantage. They have already thought about this question before asking it; it is probably a business topic with which they are already familiar. This is different from introductory or behavioral questions, where you hold more cards because the questions are about you and your experience.

Third, scenario questions are horribly open-ended. There are a million directions you could go with your answer. This fact alone can drive you nuts if you believe there is only one correct answer.

Finally, scenario questions are designed to force you to develop a response on the spot. Of course, all questions are theoretically like this. But scenario questions are different. With behavioral questions, for example, you may have to do some tweaking, depending on the way the question is asked, but you have already prepared stories that will work. But there is no practical way to rehearse responses to hundreds of potential scenario questions— that is, if you still want to have a life.

Why would interviewers put candidates through this kind of pain? Because they want to assess how you break down problems, structure your thoughts, and present solutions. They want to see how you think, and they want to see it in real time.

Here's the good news: while it isn't feasible to develop and rehearse specific answers to all possible scenario questions, you can learn a simple model that works every time. As you become familiar with and practice this model, scenario questions will become easier and easier for you. Not only will you become better at answering them, but you may also learn to enjoy them a little bit too.

Let's dive in.

The Home Base Model

In the chapter about answering behavioral questions, I used the analogy of a movie to help you understand how to develop answers. When crafting your responses using the SPAR model, you take the interviewer back to a specific place and time when you demonstrated a skill. Scenario questions require a different analogy. Instead of taking people back to a movie, you are inviting them to go on a brand-new journey with you. Together, you will explore a topic in the moment where the interviewer can see how you think and react to problems. The interviewer understands that this journey is a discovery process and that you won't have all the answers perfectly rehearsed from the beginning. They also know that you don't know from the outset what you will encounter along the way or what it will be like when you finish. All of this is perfectly okay.

What's not okay is getting lost. For example, when you go on a hike in the mountains, it's okay that you don't know what the views will be like or what animals you'll encounter. You may step in the mud or get rained on. But getting lost? Well, that's unacceptable and preventable. It's the same with scenario questions. Getting lost is the worst thing that can happen, and it happens all the time. Candidates start down a path by saying the first thing that comes to their minds, which starts them on a tangent. After a few seconds—or sometimes minutes—of talking, they look around and realize they have no idea how they've gotten where they are and no idea how to get out.

How do you not get lost? By carrying a map. You need a map in the form of a mental model to get you safely from start to finish when answering scenario questions. It's called the Home Base model. It's a simple way to structure nearly any scenario question in a way that safely guides you to the finish line. The name is derived from perhaps the simplest game ever invented: tag. In a game of tag, if I was "it," everyone would try to run away from me. When I caught someone and touched him, that kid then became "it" and we all tried to run away from him. I remember it being a tiring, chaotic free-for-all. But there was one saving grace: if I ever got too tired to keep playing, I could go to "home base" (usually a piece of playground equipment) and be safe from being tagged by anyone. At home base, I found security and rest until I was ready to get back in the game.

That is the idea behind the Home Base model. It provides a safe, reliable structure from the beginning from which you can build.

The model has three simple steps: establish a home base, explore paths, and summarize. That's it. Those three steps can help you build a two-to-five-minute answer that works every time. Here's how each component works:

Step one: establish your home base. Your home base is the core principle or idea that you will use as the foundation for your response. A good home base gives you an anchor of safety and structure. You can explore potential paths but always come back here.

Your home base needs to be broad enough to have multiple paths going out from it. For example, suppose an interviewer asks, "What do you think are some opportunities to improve our business?" One answer could be, "I think you need to improve your Facebook ads." That may be true, but where do you go from here? Nowhere, because you started too specifically, too soon. A much better answer would be, "Sure, I have a few thoughts on how to grow top-line sales. For example . . ."

Here are some more examples of how to build a good home base:

Question: How would you approach your first three months on the job?

Too specific, too soon: I would take every one of my new team members to lunch to learn about them.

Solid Home Base: My approach to coming in would be to learn, build relationships, and contribute.

• • •

Question: How would you help a customer who calls the store extremely upset because she bought our product and it stopped working after one week?

Too specific, too soon: I would refund her the money.

Solid Home Base: I would start by making sure she felt understood and listened to, then I would work to ensure that we fully resolved the problem for her.

• • •

Question: How would you go about growing a social media following for us?

Too specific, too soon: TikTok. Definitely TikTok. That's where it's at these days.

Solid Home Base: I would focus on having the right messaging for the right audience.

• • •

Question: How would you go about building your list of clients to attract to our business?

Too specific, too soon: I'd reach out to my best friend, who has several contacts in the business.

Solid Home Base: I'd focus on building relationships and getting referrals through excellent customer service.

In each of these examples, the "too specific, too soon" answers go too quickly down a specific path. They may have been good ideas, but after you say them, you have nowhere to go because you haven't yet established the foundational home base. The home base examples, on the other hand, provided a foundation strong enough on which to build your answer.

Okay, Sam, but how am I supposed to just think of a home base on the spot? I admit, this is the most difficult part of your answer. If there is any place where you should pause and take a little time to think, it is when you think of your home base. You need to get this part right because everything flows from it. Here's a trick: if you have a specific idea pop into your head, take it up a level. For example, if someone asks you how you would increase customer retention and the first idea that pops into your head is to give them money back on every purchase, take it a level up and ask yourself what you are trying to accomplish with this idea. In this case, it would be that you are trying to get loyal customers. So a good home base could be, "I would focus on developing stronger customer loyalty initiatives." If it takes you thirty seconds to think of this, it will be well worth it.

And guess what? That first idea that came into your head about giving money back can be converted into the first path you explore as part of your answer. You now have a head start on step two.

Step two: explore paths. The problem with the "too specific, too soon" examples mentioned previously isn't that they are bad ideas, it's that they are out of order. They should come after you've established a home base. For instance, in the example about building a list of clients, reaching out to a friend who has contacts in the business isn't a great home base, but it's a great path to explore against the home base of leveraging your network, building relationships, and getting referrals.

Home base: Grow top-line sales

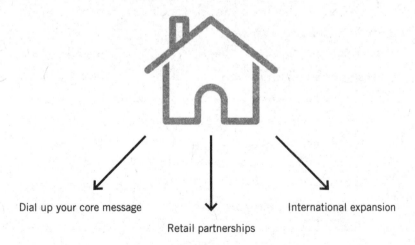

Dial up your core message   International expansion

Retail partnerships

A path is a specific idea or action you can take that ties directly back to your home base. For example, if you were asked what opportunities you see for a business, you could respond with a home base of "grow top-line sales" and follow it up with the three paths as depicted in the illustration on the previous page.

Exploring paths should be the longest part of your answer. The key word is *explore*. You shouldn't just mention the path, you should discuss it, its pros and cons and implications. This is where you demonstrate your critical thinking skills.

Let's take the example of the upset customer and build out some great paths to explore.

Question: How would you help a customer who calls in extremely upset because they bought our product and it stopped working after three days?

Home base: I would start by making sure she felt understood and listened to, then I would work to ensure that we fully resolved the problem for her.

Path One—Listening: I've found that just listening to people can help them feel better. I think it can be particularly valuable to restate what they are saying so they know we understand and even say that you would feel the same way if something like that happened to you.

Path Two—Resolving the problem: once she knows that I understand, I will assure her that I will do everything in my power to resolve the issue for her. At this point, I assume I would be familiar with the company's return policy and could offer her either a store credit or a full refund.

Path Three—Following up: I think it's really important to make sure that she feels that the problem has been resolved. After laying out our plan for her, I would ask her if she feels that this resolves the issue satisfactorily. If she says no and there is nothing else I can do for her at my level, I would reach out to my manager and let him know the situation so that he could offer suggestions or take the case over.

Step three: pick a path or summarize. Taking the time to establish a home base and explore paths has a remarkable way of giving you a great final answer to a question that you didn't have at the outset. As you explore paths, not only will your opinion materialize, but you will also have developed sound logic for it. For example, suppose you are interviewing for a social media position, and you are asked which social media platform you think is the best fit for the business. You may not have the answer right away, and that's okay. You could establish a home base that would lead to several possibilities. Then you could walk through three or four different platforms, discussing each platform's strengths and weaknesses and how they play into the business objectives. By the time you are done with your exploration, you'll likely have the answer to which platform works the best and why.

Of course, not all scenario questions ask you to choose between multiple options or have a definitive, single answer. Many scenario questions are asking simply for your opinion or approach to a problem. In these cases, it's best to summarize everything you've walked through to tie it in a bow for them. For instance, in the example where you are asked to explain how you'd deal with an upset customer who calls in, you could summarize by saying, "So, my approach would be first to listen and validate, second to do everything in my power to solve the problem, and finally to follow up to make sure that the customer is happy."

Example one

Question: You are interviewing for a job as a marketing manager for Jerry's Burgers and Fries, and you are asked, "What restaurant chain do you think is doing a really great job of marketing itself and why?"

Step one: establish a home base. *I think Chick-fil-A has done an amazing job of marketing to customers across many marketing elements.*

Step two: explore paths. *First, on the messaging side, they have a very clear focus. They recognize that they are different from all the burger places out there and they capitalize on it by being laser focused on messaging about chicken. Their campaign of cows encouraging people is the same wherever you see it, from outdoor media to college sponsorships. They really picked a lane and focused on it, which I think has led to customers understanding clearly what they are all about.*

Second, the simplicity and quality of their food is incredible. They keep options simple, but everything they offer is good quality, like whole muscle chicken breast and a unique type of fry. Even their ketchup dispensers are different and recognizable. I think this reinforces their brand promise of quality food.

Finally, I think their customer service is excellent. It's fast and friendly, and they have plenty of staff in every store. Honestly, who doesn't like to hear the words "My pleasure" after you thank someone?

Step three: pick a path or summarize. *So that's why I think Chick-Fil-A is doing such a great job: staying clear on their messaging about chicken, offering simple, high-quality food, and reinforcing that with high-quality customer service.*

Example two

Question: You are a project manager, and you get a call from one of your engineers, who tells you that there is no way the project will be delivered on time, even though senior leadership is expecting it to be completed by a certain date. How do you handle the situation?

Step one: establish a home base. *This is a tough situation for sure. On one hand, I want to keep the commitments I've made to senior leadership. I take this very seriously and pushing back a timeline is not a trivial thing. On the other hand, I want to be realistic and not burn out or lose credibility with my team, so I'd like to try to address both of these challenges in my action plan.*

Step two: explore paths. *The first thing I would do is dive deeper into the project and timeline and gain a better understanding of what happened. It's obviously a surprise that I got this phone call, but it shouldn't be, so I want to know exactly what went wrong. Also, I want to know if this is a genuine problem or if it just means that things are tight and they need some reprioritization by leadership.*

Second, if I find out that we do have a problem but that we can overcome it by reprioritizing some other tasks, I'll work with the team to make that happen so we can deliver on our timeline.

Finally, I will work with the team to develop the best possible delivery date. Then I'll craft a communication to senior leadership explaining exactly what happened and why, what we learned, and how we plan to deliver against the new timeline.

Step three: pick a path or summarize. *So, for me, it really comes down to making sure I truly understand what the reality is by working with my team and, depending on that reality, either working with my team to solve it or developing the best possible alternative solution and communicating that to senior leadership.*

Chapter Summary

Scenario questions give a real-world problem and ask you to describe how you would approach it.

They are among the hardest interview questions to answer because:

There are no right or wrong answers.

They are open-ended and ambiguous.

The interviewer has an information advantage.

They require you to think in the moment.

The way to answer them is with the Home Base model.

- Establish a home base: develop a core principle or idea that you will use as the foundation for your response.
- Explore paths: generate and discuss options that tie directly back to your home base.
- Pick a path or summarize your answer: wrap it up by offering your best choice with your reasoning. If the question does require you to pick an option, briefly summarize your home base and paths.

Preparation Checklist Progress

3–5 scenario responses (Home Base model)	
Does it start with a home base?	✔
Does it explore paths/options sufficiently?	✔
Does it either summarize learning or pick an option?	✔

eight.
know thyself

Answering Questions about You

I n 2018, Janet came to the office to get started on what seemed like a normal day at work. She was the executive vice president of consumer insights at a major consumer goods company, and a large team of marketing professionals was reporting to her. It had been three years since she joined the company, but she'd spent the prior twenty decorating her résumé at some of the most prestigious corporations in the world. On paper, Janet was a powerhouse.

But she was also mean. More than that, she was manipulative and condescending. When she met with her direct reports, she would pit them against one another, pointing out problems and asking them who was to blame. One of her employees told me that he wasn't sure if she saw anything wrong with her behavior. "She seems to get a sort of sick pleasure out of making us squirm," he said. She masked these sadistic tendencies well enough in important meetings with other departments, but a dark side came out when she was alone with her team.

One by one, Janet's team members started to report her to human resources. At first, the human resources professionals were reluctant to give any validity to the complaints and told employees that their feedback would be considered but that they should just hang in there. Time would pass and nothing would happen until eventually, month by month and year by year, the evidence became too overwhelming to ignore. Janet was a disaster for the company. Everyone could see it but her.

This is why she was so surprised when, around midmorning on that "normal" day, the human resources director in her department walked into her office with the president of the business unit, told her she was fired, and promptly walked her out of the building. As she walked through the halls that last time, her colleagues noted the look on her face: complete shock. Before she was fired, Janet had no clue her job was in danger.

People like Janet terrify employers. They are rare but are common enough and do enough damage to make companies cautious. The last thing an employer wants is to hire someone who will drain employee morale and productivity. They don't want to spend months listening to complaints, documenting them, deciding to fire someone, and consulting with legal professionals just to be sure that they can do it without losing a lawsuit.

Companies have a term for cases like Janet's and other people who get fired. The term is "poor cultural fit." Calling someone a bad cultural fit is the nicest possible way of saying that either people don't like working with that person or the person doesn't like working with everyone else. To a company, hiring a poor cultural fit is way worse than hiring someone who is incompetent. Incompetence can be solved either by training or by working around it. But there is no getting around the dumpster fire of a cultural misfit. If people can't work well with one another, it's game over.

Cultural fit will be on a hiring manager's mind when interviewing candidates. One general manager I worked for told me, "Our hiring policy is simple: no A-holes." One time, I was interviewing for a job, and after I did well in the first thirty minutes, the interviewer asked, "You're not a jerk, are you?" I could tell by the way he asked it that it was on his mind the whole interview, like he'd been holding his breath for forty-five minutes and that last question allowed him a cathartic exhale. It's on my mind every time I interview someone. I'm constantly thinking about whether the candidate is someone I would like to work with and wondering if there are any hidden bombshells I don't know about.

"You" Questions

Companies seek to combat the risk of hiring a bad cultural fit by asking "you" questions. These are direct, probing questions that require you to explain yourself as a person and professional. They are different from behavioral or scenario questions. Rather than asking you to describe how you achieved a result or how you would approach a scenario, "you" questions want you to discuss how you think about yourself. Companies ask these questions to gauge self-awareness because one common trait of difficult people is that they are unaware of just how difficult they are. Thus, if candidates can demonstrate that they are self-aware, the chances of them being extremely difficult to work with are low.

Here are some common "you" questions:

- What is your single most important accomplishment?
- What is your greatest strength?
- What is your greatest weakness?
- Where do you want to be in five years?
- Why should we hire you?

- What kind of a leader are you?
- Are you collaborative?
- What's a weird quirk you have?
- What is something you deeply believe in?
- What are you most proud of outside of work?
- What is your philosophy for dealing with difficult people?
- Why did you leave your last job?
- What kind of work do you love doing?

Do these questions make you uncomfortable? If so, you are not alone. For many, these are hard questions to answer for two reasons. First, many people genuinely don't like talking about themselves when they know they are being evaluated. Second, these questions are highly ambiguous. There is no request for a specific story. There is no specific scenario to address. It's choose your own adventure, which to many people means choose your own disaster.

The SEE Model

Fear not, there is a simple model that makes these questions easy to answer. It's a framework that works every time. The model is three letters: SEE, which stands for Statement, Explanation, Example. If you are asked a "you" question, just remember to help them SEE you. Let's look at how it works:

Statement: You start your response by giving a direct statement that succinctly answers the question. For example, if someone were to ask you, "What kind of leader are you?" your statement might be something like, "I would describe myself as results oriented, collaborative, and caring." Or, if someone were to ask you, "Where do you see yourself in five years?" your statement could be, "In five years I see myself in a manager role at this organization, with increased responsibility in scope and in people management."

The key to the statement portion is to answer the question directly without hemming and hawing. People appreciate a simple answer to a direct question. So keep it brief, concise, and related to the job. For example, if they ask, "Where do you see yourself in five years?" they don't care that you are working toward a black belt in karate (unless you are applying to be a karate instructor). The only exception to this would be if they ask you specifically for a non-professional example. For instance, I've been asked, "What is your greatest accomplishment outside of work," which, of course, is my family.

Explanation: After your simple statement, you explain what you mean by giving context that helps the interviewer better understand your answer. For example, if I were asked about my leadership style and I said that I was competitive, my explanation could have the following context: "By competitive, I mean that I have very high expectations for myself and my team. For me, it's not about beating out everyone else but about delivering work that is excellent and that I'm proud of. I suppose I'm competitive with others to a degree, but it really comes down to the expectations I have of myself." Or, if I were asked, "Why should we hire you?" and my statement said because I have the right experience, I could explain myself by saying, "My five years working on social media platforms and developing deep expertise in lead generation has set me up perfectly to add value to this job immediately."

Example: Your response now is good. Solid. Acceptable. But to make it a knockout response you need to provide proof through example. Only if you give an example will your answer be fully credible and memorable. Without an example, you will have presented strong principles that they relate to and agree with but no assurance that you actually are who you say you are.

Going back to our leadership example: if you described yourself as collaborative, you could demonstrate why that's true by saying, "For example, in my last job, I was given the 'Collaborator' award, which is a peer-nominated award given at the end of each year" or "I scheduled one-on-ones with each member of my cross-functional contacts every other week. No one else at the company was doing this at that time. It enabled me to work more efficiently than my peers because I had relationships across the organization." Examples like these provide irrefutable evidence that you are who you say you are. They also allow you to brag without looking like you are bragging.

Reframe Your Power Stories to Fit the SEE Model

The good news about answering most "you" questions is that you don't need to develop completely new stories for them because your power examples still apply. You merely need to put them through the SEE model instead of the SPAR model. For example, an interviewer might ask, "Can you tell me about a time you had to persuade someone to your way of thinking?" or "What is your philosophy about persuading other people to your way of thinking?" One is a behavioral question and the other is a "you" question. But the story you tell is the same.

In chapter 6, we covered behavioral questions. One of the questions was, "Tell me about a time when you had to persuade others to your way of thinking?" Here is a summary of that SPAR story:

Situation: I was working as a marketing intern for a clothing retailer and was asked to figure out a way to boost online sales.

Problem: I encountered a lot of opposition from the in-store buyers.

Action: To solve this, I did three things:

I set up time with the key players of the in-store buying group to listen to their concerns and build relationships.

I researched and used data to show that online and in-store buyers could actually boost one another's sales, not hurt them.

Before my final presentation, I showed each of them my recommendations to make sure they had a voice.

Result: I was able to make a compelling presentation to company executives with the full support of the buying group.

Now let's look at how we can use that exact same story to answer a "you" question. Suppose that, instead of asking, "Tell me about a time you had to persuade someone to your way of thinking," the interviewer asks, "What is your philosophy on persuading other people at work?" Here's what your reframed answer could look like:

Statement: When I try to persuade people, I do it by building a personal relationship first and then persuading through facts.

Explanation: I start by building a personal relationship because it builds a foundation of trust. I've found it's hard to get someone to listen to me if they don't know me or trust me. And the reason I like using facts when trying to persuade is that it shows that I don't have a personal agenda and that I'm just trying to get to the answer that will be best for the business.

Example: One example of this from my work experience is when I worked as a marketing intern for a clothing retailer and was responsible for boosting our online sales. The in-store buying group was afraid that I was going to steal a lot of their sales, so they weren't supportive of what I was doing. To get them on board, I set up a time to meet with each of them and listened to their concerns to build trust. Then I showed them some research I'd done that demonstrated that online sales could actually boost in-store sales. After that, they were highly supportive of me.

You see! Same story, different frameworks.

Common "You" Questions

Let's dive into examples of how to apply the SEE model to five common "you" questions.

What is your greatest strength?

This is a very common question and the SEE model works great with it. But before busting out your statement, consider two things. First, they aren't really asking you, "What is your greatest strength?" They are asking you, "What is your greatest strength *as it pertains to this position?*" They don't want to hear about your shopping skills or your CrossFit performance or Minecraft creations. They want to hear only about things that are relevant to the job matter unless they specifically ask for something outside of work. Second, steer clear of overly general strengths. Strengths like "I work extremely hard" or "I am charismatic" typically aren't specific enough to provide tangible evidence for the interviewer.

Here's what a good answer to this question looks like in the SEE format. Suppose you are asked this question in a job interview, and you know analytical thinking is an important part of the role.

Statement: One of my greatest strengths is my analytical ability.

Explanation: I have always had an interest in data and have recently become particularly good at breaking it down into simple insights so that better business decisions can be made.

Example: For example, I recently worked for an online clothing retailer as a business analyst. My boss asked me to help her better understand our inventory position for our baby clothes line. Up until that point, no one on the team knew how much inventory we had, which created all sorts of out-of-stocks and missed sales opportunities, so I built a model that tracked inventory movements anytime we got a sale or made a new purchase. The model had a simple dashboard that helped people understand exactly how much new inventory, by size, they should order each week to stay in stock and maximize sales. That model saved the company hundreds of thousands of dollars and is still in use today.

This is a solid answer. My statement is concise and not too general, and it's relevant to many jobs. My explanation gives a little more context and tees up my example nicely. Then my example provides irrefutable proof that I have strong analytical skills.

Here's another example. This time you are interviewing as an account manager for an advertising agency, and you know client-service skills are important for the job.

Statement: I'm very good at working well with a variety of personality types.

Explanation: I've always been highly interested in people and what makes them tick. This has allowed me to understand and adapt to other people's communication styles.

Example: For example, in my last job, one of our biggest customers could be very difficult to work with. He complained a lot and often threatened to take his business elsewhere. He burned through three customer service reps at our company before they assigned him to me. When I started working with him, I quickly realized that he didn't really want to take his business elsewhere, but he threatened to do it because he didn't feel like he was getting the attention he deserved. He just wanted someone to listen to him and make him feel important, so I created a system of proactively reaching out to him periodically before he got anxious. I emailed him and sometimes called him weekly to let him know the latest news on his account. Within a few months, he was a happy customer.

What is your greatest weakness?

This question is the evil twin of "What is your greatest strength?" Many get nervous about answering this question because they believe they might share a weakness that will disqualify them from getting the job. It's a valid concern. When crafting your answer to this question you certainly don't want to give an egregious weakness like, "I just don't really like people, and most of the time I want to be alone" or I "lose my temper at work" or "I hate the sound of children laughing." But most people are smart enough to steer clear of mentioning those weaknesses. The more common mistake candidates make is giving a weakness that isn't really a weakness, like "I'm a perfectionist" or "I just care too much" or "I serve and sacrifice for my people to a fault." Interviewers almost always will see these answers for what they are—strengths disguised as weaknesses—and your response won't land.

The way to answer this question is to come up with a reasonable work-related weakness and then talk about what you are doing to address it. A reasonable weakness could sound like this: "I sometimes get bogged down in the details and need to remember to take a step back and see the big picture." Or it could sound like this: "I am a numbers-oriented person, which has its benefits, but it also means that the opportunity for me to improve is to build my 'intuition muscle' a bit more."

That would be your statement. For your explanation, you'd talk about the implications of your weakness. This makes you relatable and demonstrates your self-awareness. And, for your example, you'd give one specific way in which you are working to address it.

Statement: I am an action-oriented person, which is usually a good thing. However, that bias for action and my zeal to get something done sometimes lead me to skip some important details.

Explanation: As a result, I've noticed that that can sometimes make those of my team members who are a little more conservative or detail oriented uncomfortable.

Example: One thing that I've tried to do is seek the advice of those team members who I know are more detail oriented and conservative before moving forward with a big business decision. Just last week, a critical business decision needed to be made. My natural inclination was to just move forward, but instead I called two of my peers to run it by them, and sure enough, they pointed out a couple of additional things I needed to do before continuing. It made my ultimate decision a lot better.

This is a fantastic answer. I gave a reasonable weakness in my statement. I showed self-awareness by pointing out the implications in my explanation, and finally, I gave a specific example of how I'm trying to address the weakness.

How would you describe your leadership style?

Answering this question should be a quick reframe if you have a couple of leadership SPAR stories in your back pocket. Also, when interviewers ask questions like "What is your leadership style?" or "How good are you at working with people?" you have the option of picking more than one of your attributes. This means that you can use the SEE model more than once, in sequence, in your answer. In this case, your statement will set up however many attributes you highlight, and then you'll separate the attributes as you do your explanation and examples.

Here's how it works:

Statement: I would say that my leadership style is results oriented and collaborative.

Explanation one (results oriented): Regarding my drive for results, I have high expectations of myself and my team. I like to lay out ambitious goals, and I do everything I can to hit them.

Example one (results oriented): In my last role, our team was the number one sales team at the company for nine out of the last twelve months. I set that goal specifically for my team, and we tracked it every week. We achieved our goal by staying focused.

Explanation two (collaborative): But I also recognize that the way results are achieved is important. It should be done in a way that enables others to succeed and contribute. Otherwise, you burn people out quickly.

Example two (collaborative): One thing I've tried to do with each of my team members in my last role is to have weekly one-on-one meetings where I ask them how they feel they are contributing, what their concerns are, and what I can be doing better to help them. Sticking to these one-on-one meetings has enabled me to maintain trust with my team, listen to them, and let them know that we're all in this together.

Where do you see yourself in two, three, four, five years? Before answering this question, reframe it as if they were asking, "Where do you see yourself at this company in two, three, four, five years?" Do some research on people who are in the same department for which you are applying and who have been at the company for a while. See what their jobs are like because it will give you clues to what you will be doing in a few years. If it doesn't sound attractive to you, you may be applying for the wrong job. Maybe you just want to do this job for two years and then go work on your own. That's fine, but (1) that's not what they want to hear, and (2) you don't know that for sure. So approach these questions by trusting that there is a decent chance you could stay there for five years.

Here's an example. Let's assume you are applying for a job as a buyer at PetSmart.

Statement: In five years, I can see myself growing within an organization like PetSmart with increased responsibility and impact.

Explanation: That means I would be buying bigger and more impactful categories and gaining a much greater understanding of the business and how I can grow it.

Example: For example, I see myself having learned the basics of how to think about business trends in the pet food space, how to analyze the P&L [profit and loss statement] with all of the relevant levers, and finally having some good team management experience and increasingly growing with my team.

These are goals the company would likely have for you, which means you've got yourself a good answer.

Why do you want to work here?

You have probably already answered this question if you've done a good job in your introductory statement. But in case you are asked it again, the way to answer is to think like a matchmaker. For a match to work, both parties have to give something and get something from the deal, so you want to think about the unique things that you can contribute and also the unique things you will gain with this job. For example, suppose you are applying for a job as an e-commerce manager for an online clothing retailer.

Statement: I want to work here because it would mean I can take my retail background to the next level by applying it to the tech industry.

Explanation: I have a lot of experience in merchandising clothes from my time in the retail industry. I have developed a good pulse about what customers like to see and how they like to see it. I know how to make the products look attractive and to price them right, which I think can be a major asset to this company. But I also think that there is a lot I can learn.

Example: Specifically, I think I could learn a lot about your email marketing strategies. I have been a customer of your company for five years, and I think your email campaigns are amazing—super eye-catching and always engaging to read. I also feel like you don't send me too many emails as compared to your competitors. Email marketing is an area that I'd like to learn more about, and I think this is the perfect organization for accomplishing that.

Chapter Summary

"You" questions are those that ask you to talk about yourself and how you think.

Companies ask "you" questions to gauge your self-awareness and cultural fit for the company.

You don't need to develop new stories to answer these questions; you merely need to reframe the power stories you already have.

Put your stories into the SEE model:

- Statement: give a simple, concise answer to their question.
- Explanation: explain what you mean by giving more context.
- Example: provide an example that proves your point.

Preparation Checklist Progress

3–5 "you" responses (SEE Model)	
Do each have a statement, explanation, and example?	✔

nine.

avoid land mines

Handling Illegal, Negative,
or Just Plain Wacky Questions

Welcome to the job interview question frontier! Up to this point in the book, we've been living in a civilized world where job interview questions have logical reasons and good intentions. They are based on the skills listed in the job description. They are asked under the assumption that you will have great responses that will make them want to hire you. This understanding of the civilized world has enabled you to anticipate and master these questions with excellent responses. If you've put in the work, you have successfully conquered this world.

But you are now on the job interview frontier, where anything can happen. In this world, interviewers can ask you questions they really shouldn't be asking. Questions that have nothing to do with the job description. Questions that are designed with the sole purpose of derailing you or making you nervous. Questions that even the interviewers don't know why they are asking. Even questions that are illegal. In the frontier, the job interviewers themselves can be terribly inexperienced, sadistic, or moronic. It's a strange place, this frontier.

In my opinion, most of the questions we'll cover in this chapter aren't useful to the hiring decisions. But that doesn't matter. What matters is that they do occasionally get asked, so you should be prepared to answer them well, with poise and confidence. For example, if an interviewer were to ask you, "So, how far along are you in your pregnancy?" or "What did you dislike about your last boss?" or "Do you prefer cats or dogs?" or "Why are you quitting your current job?" how would you respond? Would you be caught off guard, or would you have the confidence to face these questions head-on?

This chapter will teach you to hold your own with these questions. We'll cover four types of questions: trap questions, which are seemingly genuine questions that have the potential to take you to a negative place; on-the-spot creativity questions, which require you to offer creative ideas in real time; illegal questions, which force you to make the difficult decision whether to answer the question or call out the interviewer; and wacky questions, which are so strange they almost make you want to laugh out loud. Each of these question types is different, but they are grouped together in one chapter because they share a common theme: they catch people off guard and have the potential to fluster and derail candidates. I'm going to prepare you for these questions by giving you several examples and working through potential responses for each one. I hope you don't encounter any of these questions. I think it's likely that you won't. But I promised I'd prepare you for everything, so let's go.

Trap Questions

Trap questions are seemingly harmless at first, but the more you try to answer them, the more you realize they have the potential to blow up your interview. For example, "Why are you leaving your current job?" seems like a reasonable question until you realize that some of your reasons could make you look overly negative or cynical. "What did you like least about your last manager?" appears like an innocent question about your working style until you realize it creates the potential to trash your old boss. That's why these are called trap questions. They seem genuine—and they may be— but they have the potential to put you in a box that you don't want to be in.

Why do interviewers ask trap questions? Who knows! Sometimes they genuinely want to know more about you and your career intentions and believe these questions will help. This is especially true if you haven't fully explained your career intentions during your opening statement. For example, if you haven't explained exactly why this new position is perfect for your career, they may ask, "Why are you leaving your current job?" Other times, they may be skeptical about your candidacy and want to dig deeper to see if their skepticism is valid. In the most extreme cases, they may just take sick pleasure in asking you a difficult question and watching you squirm.

Let's look at some examples.

Why are you leaving your current job?

This one has the potential to lure you into talking negatively about your last company. Don't take the bait! You don't need to say anything bad about your company to produce a great response.

Bad-mouthing your past organization says more about you than it does the organization. Instead, tell them what you enjoyed about your last position and then flip the discussion to the current job, highlighting something that the current job has that your past job didn't, like different experience, more responsibility, or more impact.

Example One: I've really enjoyed the technical skills I learned through my current position, but the scope with which I could apply those skills was relatively limited. One of the things that gets me so excited about this new role is that I can take those skills I've learned and apply them on a bigger playing field.

Example Two: My last job had a great culture and people I loved working with, but there were limited opportunities for growth. What gets me so excited about this role is the potential to grow into new responsibilities and skills.

Example Three: My current job was a great fit for me up until now. Given that it's a large corporation, I got to work on things that had a lot of scale. But my individual impact on key decisions wasn't as strong as I wanted it to be because the company was so big. That's why I'm so excited about this position because I feel the next step for my career is to work for a smaller, more scrappy company where I can guide the ship and really influence things for the better.

What didn't you like about your last boss?

This question is the evil twin of the last one, in that it creates the potential for unattractive negativity. This is different from conflict. It's okay to highlight conflict in your responses to demonstrate how you resolve it. But any time you start to blame or attack, you enter the unattractive negativity danger zone. Even if your boss was a raging psychopath and the only reason you are applying for a new job is to get away from them, you must find a way to show that you can work with others. So instead of merely saying something you didn't like about your last manager, discuss a point of conflict and how you got through it.

Example One: My last boss and I had a great relationship, but sometimes we approached projects differently. I was much more concerned with the big picture and hitting deadlines, and she was concerned with making sure all the details were right, even to the point where she would edit my words on PowerPoint slides. Sometimes this made things difficult when we were on a tight timeline, so I had to adjust my style a bit to make things work. I started to build in "buffer" time, an extra two to three days, before a deadline to allow my boss to chime in and provide feedback on my work. At first, this felt like a major inconvenience, but over time I saw the value in it. It helped me feel more prepared when I presented major milestones to executives. It also helped me be more detail oriented because I knew if I wasn't, she would correct my errors anyway. Without our different styles, I wouldn't have grown in the way I have.

Example Two: My last boss has an extremely "hands-off" working style because he was so busy. In my first three months of working at the company, I saw him only once and received only a few emails from him. This was a struggle for me because I was trying to establish myself at my new organization and felt like my manager wasn't there to help me. So I decided to be proactive by sending weekly emails to him, telling him exactly what I was working on and asking for his feedback. At first, I wasn't getting responses, but eventually he started giving me quick pieces of feedback on direction via email. Pretty soon, he was giving me more assignments. Within a couple of months, I was a critical member of his team and interacted with him daily.

What type of work did you most dislike doing at your last job?

This is another negativity trap. While these questions may seem like an opportunity to complain, you should use them to explain your personal growth journey. You can also use them to point out the virtues of the job for which you are interviewing. Here are a couple of examples:

Example One: There was a lot of administrative work associated with my last job. I was required to do a lot of reporting on my business. The work was necessary but tedious and not highly impactful on the business. I much preferred the part of my job where I could strategize about the future and develop ideas for new products. To manage through the parts of my work I didn't like, I automated as much as I could without sacrificing quality. I borrowed ideas from people who

really enjoyed the reporting aspect of the job, and they frequently jumped in and helped me. I eventually got it to a
point where I was doing the reporting piece of my job well
but in about half the time, which freed me up to do more of
the high-impact things that I enjoyed. It was all because I
focused on efficiency, and I got other people who were passionate about that type of work to help me.

Example Two: My last job had a lot of seasonality to it, so it
would get extremely busy and stressful during the holidays.
Don't get me wrong, I'm not afraid of hard work, but the
intense spikes in the business in peak season were difficult on
my family. Candidly, one of the reasons I am so interested in
this position is that this business seems to have a more consistent workload throughout the year, which will be a great fit
for me.

Who did you get along with least in your last position and why?

This question is yet another opportunity to talk about how you
overcome differences in working styles, to show how you resolve
conflict without being overly negative.

Example One: I'm in marketing, so part of my job is to take
some calculated risks to move the business forward. But one
of my counterparts in the legal department was very risk
averse, so we were often at odds when it came to new marketing campaigns. This made it really challenging because I
felt like everything I tried got rejected by the legal department. Ultimately, it was a process of making my case for

why I felt like my ideas should be approved, and if they weren't approved, I would escalate the situation to my manager, who would help me navigate the situation. But I always made it a point to be respectful and never make it personal, even though we disagreed on key business decisions. To this day, we are good friends even though, organizationally, we are at odds.

Example Two: I worked with someone in my last job who was overly concerned with who got credit for work, and sometimes she would take credit for work she didn't do. I think she was worried that if she didn't get the credit she deserved, she wouldn't excel at the company. The problem was that most people could sense that she wanted to take credit for things, and the very thing that she hoped would help her reputation was hurting it. I decided to be nice but firm. If I had genuinely done the work for something and she took credit from me, I would have a conversation with her and stick up for myself. Sometimes she didn't like those conversations, but I was always kind about it, and it created a good boundary. Eventually, she became fairer minded about things, and we grew to really respect one another.

On-the-Spot Creativity Questions

Sometimes, interviewers will ask questions to test your ability to be creative in real time. These are different from behavioral questions where they ask you for a time when you thought outside the box or when you had to use creativity to solve a problem. No, these questions will put your creativity to the test on the spot. For example, they could ask you to brainstorm a new product line, to find five different ways to sell something, or to position a product in different ways. These questions are more common for marketing, design, and other creative roles. It's impossible to prepare for the exact questions you'll be asked, of course. But that doesn't mean you can't become great at answering them. You can as you become more familiar with and practice them.

For example, suppose you are in an interview and the hiring manager pulls out a pen from her pocket and says, "Give me as many ways to position this pen for sale as fast as you can." This prompt may freak you out a little bit, but there is no need for concern. It's nothing more than a rapid-fire brainstorm. They are giving you license to have fun with it and say what first comes to mind. Here are some things you could say:

- You could use it as a weapon and market it as a self-defense tool for women in cities.
- It could be a luxury pen with gold-colored ink, and you could call it "liquid gold."
- It could be a trick pen that doesn't work and that frustrates the heck out of people.
- It could be used as a walking stick for tiny little gnomes.
- You could get a celebrity to endorse it as a limited edition.
- You could market it as a finger baton, with the perfect weight balance to twirl it between your fingers when you are bored.
- You could market it as a one-time-use pen that is disposable after one note is written.
- It could be the most environmentally sound pen in the world, made of paper and 100 percent biodegradable.

I admit, these aren't the most amazing ideas in the world, but the questions didn't ask for amazing. It asked for as many ideas as possible as fast as possible. These answers would work well for this question, but hundreds of other answers could work as well.

You may be thinking to yourself, "I can't answer these because I'm just not that creative." Wrong! You are creative. Creativity is not reserved only for those who do interpretive dance or oil paintings. It's about solving problems, something every human is required to do every day just to survive life. The key is to let go of the inner "I'm not creative" voice, and let your ideas flow.

Sometimes it's difficult to know how to get started with your answers. In these cases, I've found it helpful to ask myself an additional question to the one they are asking. For example, if someone asks me for several ways to market a pen, I could ask a couple of additional questions of myself, like "Who might this pen be for" or "Who uses pens the most today?" or "Who never uses pens but should?" These questions could jolt my creative, problem-solving brain better than if I were just thinking about the pen itself.

Here are some more examples with sample responses.

Give me three ways you would sell a TV to a blind person.

1. *It's the best-sounding TV on the market, with rich tones and . . .*

2. *It could be a gift for a friend or family member that isn't blind.*

3. *It would be a TV that came with narration, so not only could you hear the people speaking, but if there were amazing visual elements, the narration would call out*

what is going on, like, "Beautiful, handsome man appears"
or "Massive explosion on the boat!"

You work at a donut shop, and you are trying to grow
sales. Tell me five different types of donuts you could
create and why you think they'd sell.

1. *A salted caramel donut. That seems to be a popular flavor*
   right now.
2. *A dark chocolate donut made with Godiva chocolate.*
   You know, for the older crowd with more sophisticated
   taste.
3. *Custom-made donuts that you could write a message on,*
   like "Happy Birthday, Jenny," or "You deserve this."
4. *Emoji donuts, for example, with a thumbs-up emoji or*
   heart emoji.
5. *Donuts that have pictures of celebrities or political figures*
   on them.

Again, it's not about a correct answer, it's about having fun and
letting your mind go. Practice a few of these, and you'll find that
you really enjoy these questions!

Illegal Questions

Several questions are against the law to ask, like direct questions
related to your race, age, gender, country of origin, marital status,
or religion. There are, however, questions that are perfectly legal but
overlap with illegal questions. For example, someone can't ask you
how old you are, but they can ask you if you are at least eighteen if
it's part of the job requirements. They can't ask you if you are a US

citizen, but they can ask you if you are legally eligible to work in the United States. They can't ask you if you have a disability or medical conditions, but they can ask you if you are able to lift fifty pounds on a regular basis as part of the job. They can't ask you what your native language is, but they can ask you if you speak Spanish. These requirements should be on the job description so it shouldn't be a huge surprise when you are asked about them.

In most cases, interviewers who ask an illegal question don't even realize they are doing it. Many are simply undertrained and inexperienced. Nevertheless, being asked an illegal question leaves you with the conundrum of how to respond. When I'm asked by clients how they should answer an illegal question, my answer is always, "Tell me more," because these questions are unique to each situation, and I need to understand the context in which the question is asked to craft the right strategy. Only they can determine if the intent is malicious or benign, or if the question seems like it was asked by accident or on purpose, or how they believe your answer will affect their candidacy. I can't do that for clients, but I can tell them that they are under no obligation to answer an illegal question in a certain way. I can also provide options.

For example, if someone asks you what country you were born in, here are three ways you could answer the question.

Option One: Ask the interviewer the reason for the question. This is a potential way to remind them the question is illegal, or at least inappropriate, without telling them directly. I simply smile and ask, "Oh, is there a reason for that question?"

Option Two: Ask the interviewer how the question pertains to the job description. This is like option one, but different in that it keeps it more focused on actual job requirements. It sets a boundary by reminding the interviewer that questions should be focused on assessing the skills required by the position.

Option Three: Tell them, straight up, that their question is illegal. It's more confrontational but will leave no misunderstandings. One downside of calling out an interviewer directly is that it may embarrass or annoy them. That may be fine, and I'm not saying you shouldn't call them out, especially if they are knowingly asking an illegal question. But, in my experience, if it's an honest mistake, there is no need to dwell on an interviewer's mistake and make a big deal out of it. It all comes down to how you respond and to the nonverbal expressions that make a big difference. You and I know there is a difference between tersely stating, "Excuse me, that is an illegal question!" and kindly saying, "I don't mean to be rude or to derail this interview, but I believe that question is illegal."

Option Four: Just answer the question. Another downside of directly calling out the interviewer is that it could make it look like you have something to hide. Again, I'm not saying it's right that they ask an illegal question or that it's always best to answer an illegal question. But sometimes it is, especially if you believe the question is harmless. For example, if someone asked me what year I graduated from high school as part of interview small talk about high school sports, I'd tell him that I graduated in 1999. And if someone were to ask me where I'm from, I'd promptly respond, "Walnut

Creek, California." I recognize that as an American going for a job in America, it is easier for me to answer that question. I only bring these examples up to demonstrate that context matters and sometimes just answering the questions is the way to go.

Wacky Questions

Some interviewers ask questions that are plain weird. Why? Sometimes, it's to throw you off your game to see how you will react. Other times, it's the belief that a crazy question brings out your true, unfiltered self and they'll be able to get to know you better. And other times, well, I have no idea.

Regardless of why they ask such questions, there is no need to be rattled by them. Weird questions rarely have a "correct" answer, and they give you license to have a little fun. Don't act like you are caught off guard and don't know how to answer the question. Instead, play along with confidence. For example, if someone asks you, "If you were stuck on a desert island with nothing but food and water, how would you spend your time?" you could say, "I'd focus my time on becoming as fit as I possibly can be and would work out for hours a day so that when I get off the island, people wouldn't even recognize me. Since I'm goal oriented, this would help keep my mind on a worthy goal and off the fact that I'm stuck on an island with nowhere to go." And that would be a perfectly good answer.

The only way you could screw up your answer is if you don't provide any explanation. Anytime you give an answer to a weird question, it should always include a "because." For example, "I prefer green over blue because I think it has always looked better on me with my skin tone." Or "Rocky Balboa is of course better than Apollo Creed because he had all the endurance even though he wasn't flashy." A pretty good answer, but as a bonus you can tie it back to you and how you relate to the job description. You could add, "I always liked Rocky better because he wasn't flashy but had endurance. That's how I try to be in my work. Always dependable, always willing to work harder, any talent I lack I try to make up for with grit and determination."

Many wacky questions can't be reasonably tied back to the job description, and that's okay. More than anything, if you get a crazy question, just answer honestly. Here are some examples and how I'd answer them personally.

What is your favorite song to sing Karaoke to?

Anything Ke$ha is a solid choice. There is a lot of shock value when a forty-two-year-old man like me gets up and is willing to sing something from her. I like those songs because they are fast-paced and absurd, which is basically the goal of karaoke.

What would you do if you won $10 million?

Well, sorry to be boring, but I'd first pay off my house because I want the feeling of having no mortgage. After that, my wife and I would probably want to travel a bit. I'd also like to start tipping well and maybe surprising people who I think could need some cash. This would leave me with over $9.5 million, and I have no idea what I'd do with the rest! Maybe I could become an angel investor or maybe I'd just put it in the bank until I feel strongly that I should do something with it.

Who is your favorite superhero?

It's a cross between Batman and Iron Man. Both have something in common in that they don't have any supernatural powers—Batman for my bad-mood self and Iron Man for my good-mood self. But I really like them both because they attained superhero status by using their natural brains and ingenuity. In that sense, they are relatable and approachable. I could almost be Iron Man or Batman and that excites me.

What is your spirit animal?

It's a golden retriever because I like to think I'm eager to do the right thing and can work well with just about any other animal. I'm friendly and gregarious, even if it means I'm a little too casual sometimes. I also assume the best in people, including the assumption that they will like me once they get to know me.

If you could have any superpower, what would it be?

Honestly, I don't like the idea of a superpower because it feels a little bit like cheating in life to me. But if I could have one, I think it would be cool to speak any language. I like the idea of being able to communicate with any person on earth at any time. It would make me feel like the ultimate human. Maybe that's not technically a superpower, but it sure feels like one.

Do you prefer cats or dogs?

Dogs for sure. What dog doesn't love when you come home and want to please you? What dog doesn't want to hang out with you? They are built-in buddies, kind of like a child. Cats, on the other hand, while easier to take care of, often want to be alone and are fiercely independent.

If someone were to write your biography, what would it be titled?

Hmmm. Well, I suppose it should be called, My Family Runs My Life. I think it would be about how blessed I am to come from and to have built the family that I have. It would be about the power of family bonds and why the sacrifices we make for relatives are worth it.

Where would you never want to travel?

I've heard enough about the Philippines to be officially scared. A friend of mine went there and got sick and I've never forgotten that. Don't get me wrong, I'd love to meet the people and see the culture there, but the fear of getting sick puts it pretty darn far down on my list.

Chapter Summary

In the job interview frontier, you may get asked the following types of questions:

- Trap questions, which are seemingly genuine questions that have the potential to take you to an overly negative place.

Answer them by staying positive and discussing how you overcame a difficult situation.

- On-the-spot creativity questions, which require you to offer ideas in real time.

Answer them by staying calm and playing along. Don't worry about having a perfect answer.

- Illegal questions, which force you to make a difficult decision to answer the question or call out the interviewers.

Answer them by asking the purpose behind the question, asking how the question applies to the job description, telling them the question is illegal, or just answering the question. It depends on the context of the question.

- Wacky questions, which are strange enough to make you want to laugh out loud.

Answer them by having fun and being confident. Recognize that there is no one "right answer" and that strange questions allow for strange answers.

Preparation Checklist Progress

Prepare for land mines	
Trap questions	✔
On-the-spot creativity questions	✔
Illegal questions	✔
Wacky questions	✔

ten.
strike last, strike hard

Asking Questions, Closing, and Following Up

I n the fall of 2007, I flew to Minneapolis to interview for an internship with Target Corporation at its corporate headquarters. The interview process was the most rigorous I'd ever seen up to that point in my life. It included formal interviews with two executives, a lunch interview with a junior-level employee, and two online tests, one of them a personality test with questions like "Are you afraid of snakes?" and "Do you secretly compete with other vehicles on the road while driving?" And, if that wasn't strange enough, the interview process required me to meet with their in-house psychologist after my online tests to psychoanalyze me in person!

I flew back home exhausted, and a few days later, I was notified by email that I didn't get the internship. As is almost always the case, they gave me no reasons for the rejection. Maybe it was that I wasn't a great fit for the company or maybe the shrink declared me mentally unstable. But I think the real reason I didn't get the offer had more to do with my interview with one of the executives. This man ran the internship program at Target and was clearly the head decision-maker regarding incoming interns. It was obvious by his quick pace and the comfort level with which he asked his questions that he had interviewed a lot of people over the years. He asked about my experience level and my test scores at business school and my reasons for wanting to work at Target. The interview seemed to be going okay when he said, "Well, Sam, thanks for coming in, I appreciate the time. I think the only thing that makes me question you as an intern is your level of experience."

Suddenly, I felt exposed. He was right that my experience was a little light. I didn't come from the retail industry, and I only had two years of pre–business school experience as opposed to the average of three to five years. I was caught completely off guard by his question and didn't know what to say. The only thing I could think to do was smile and say, "I can understand that." And with that, the executive kindly concluded the interview and shuffled me along to my next appointment. After I was denied the internship, I realized that I had missed an opportunity to finish my interview strong. He had brought up a legitimate concern, and I didn't resolve it. To this day, I believe that my failure to close that interview strong was the reason I didn't get the internship. That, or the fact that I am, indeed, afraid of snakes.

Finishing your interview strong is almost as important as starting it strong. It's an opportunity to tie things in a bow and agree on the next steps. In this chapter, we'll cover how to finish your interview strong by asking great questions, resolving concerns, and reinforcing your interest in the position. We'll also cover how to nail down the next steps so you both know what to expect in the weeks after your interview.

Ask Engaging Questions

When interviewers allow you to ask questions toward the end of your interview, you should take it as a good sign. It often means that the interview is going well and they want to give you the opportunity to learn more about the company and even sell you a bit on the job—not a bad position to be in.

But don't misunderstand. This is not your opportunity to cross-examine the interviewer and fully vet the company, nor is it the time to resolve your concerns by getting every detail you need to make a final decision. Remember, you are still in an interview and are being evaluated. You don't have an offer yet. I'm all for getting the information you need to make a sound decision but not when you've been given five minutes to ask questions at the end of an interview. Speaking with the hiring manager again is easy and often standard procedure after you have a written offer. But during the interview, focus on asking questions that will lead to an impressive, engaging, and positive conversation.

Here are some types of questions that you should avoid entirely in the interview. If you really want to ask them, you should wait until you have an offer:

1. **Questions you ask only to look smart and informed.**
   The problem with asking questions only to impress is that you run the risk of asking questions that have nothing to do with the job description and that the interviewer can't answer. For example, if you are applying for a job in operations and you ask, "I noticed in your financial statement that your balance sheet increased by 30 percent year over year. What do you

think is driving that?" not only will the interviewer have no clue how to answer it, but the answer won't be useful to you.

2. **Questions you ask that clearly put your career desires first.** Questions like "What is the work-life balance like at this company?" or "How long does it typically take to get promoted in this position?" create the potential for you to look like a selfish employee. To be clear, you should be selfish. This is your career. There's nothing wrong with work-life balance and career advancement. Both of those things are clear priorities for me when considering a job. But it's tacky to ask at the end of an interview.

3. **Questions that require the interviewer to speculate.** You don't want to put the interviewer on the spot. Asking speculative questions, like the future earnings of the company or if layoffs are coming, will do just that.

4. **Negative questions.** Avoid questions like "What do you dislike the most about this job?" and "What are the worst parts of the culture here?" and "Your company has had some terrible online reviews. Can you address those?" You want the conversation to be optimistic. Asking something negative only creates the potential for either a downer conversation or a situation where the interviewer is concerned that you are a pessimist. If you really want to know the answer to these questions, save them for after you have an offer or after you are in the job.

5. **Questions that require long, complicated answers.** It's okay for a question to challenge the interviewer, but it's

not okay to give her a chore. For example, don't ask her to map out strategies in detail or list things in order of priority. It's okay for an interview to feel like a test for you, but not for your interviewer. She wants to feel like she's engaged in a conversation, not taking a test.

6. **Questions to which the interviewer likely doesn't know the answer.** But even if you really want to know about a product recall or a balance sheet write-off, your interviewer will likely be at a loss if they don't work in that department. So keep your questions related to the job description and function for which you're applying.

Finally, don't go over the allocated interview time unless you have permission from the interviewer. If time is limited but the interviewer still asks you if you have questions, reinforce the fact that you want to be respectful of time and let the interviewer give you permission to continue. Otherwise, end on time.

So how do you ask impressive, engaging, and positive questions while avoiding the types of questions listed previously? Generally, you are in the safe zone if you follow the guidance laid out in chapter 2 on informational interviews. If you ask questions that (1) you are genuinely interested in, (2) are related to the job, and (3) the interviewer is uniquely positioned to answer, you're on the right track. It also doesn't hurt to ask questions that show you've done some research and want to do well at the job should you be given an offer. These parameters are highly likely to engage you and the interviewer in a dialogue because you'll both be interested in the topic, and the interviewer will feel useful. Here are some examples of great questions to ask.

- What are your most successful employees like?
- What are the biggest challenges and opportunities facing you right now?
- Can you tell me what excites you most about working here?
- I noticed your team recently launched a new product. What are you most excited about and what keeps you up at night regarding the launch?
- How would you describe the culture in this department and how do you think it could be improved?
- Tell me about your vision for your team. What do you want to see happen over the next couple of years or more?
- What are some of the most important things you're looking for someone in this role to accomplish in the first few months?
- Tell me about your career path and how you got to where you are now.

Resolve Concerns with "I Understand" and "However . . ."

One of the questions you ask the interviewer should be reserved for finding out if the interviewer has any lingering concerns. Sometimes you'll have a clue that there is a concern by something the interviewer has said or by the way things felt during one of your responses. Other times, you'll have no idea because the interview seemed to go so well. Either way, never let an interview conclude without attempting to resolve concerns.

There are various ways to do this, each with varying degrees of intensity. The level of directness depends on the context of the interview, the rapport you've built with the interviewer, and how you've felt each of your responses was received. The most direct approach, for example, would be to ask, "Now that you've had a chance to interview me, how do you feel about me as a candidate?" It's a good approach but maybe puts the interviewer a little too much on the spot. A less intense approach would be to refer to a specific point in the interview that you'd like to return to and say, "I noticed that you seemed concerned with my answer about process improvement. Do you have a concern about that answer that I can address?" If you felt the interview went fine but just want to be sure, you could say, "Are there any remaining questions or concerns you have about my candidacy that I haven't answered?"

No matter how direct you choose to be, the way you answer the question is always the same. Whatever concern they highlight, use the words "I understand" and "however" in your response. Here's how it works:

Concern: You've only been in your current job for eight months. That's not a lot of time before deciding to jump ship.

Response: I can understand how that would be a concern. It's fair that you'd want someone who is committed for a longer time. I will say, however, that I do believe my other experiences demonstrate my level of commitment. For example, I held my previous job for five years. The short time in my current job was really driven by the fact that the job turned out to be different from what was in the description in several ways. I enjoy the job and could stay there, but it doesn't provide the same type of experience that this job does, which is exactly what I'm looking for.

. . .

Concern: Most of your experience has been working for large corporations. Working for a start-up is a different animal, and a lot of people have a difficult time making the transition. How do you think you'd do in a start-up environment?

Response: I can understand that a lot of people don't transition well. I have a lot of friends who went from big to small and struggled. For me, however, I think there are some indicators that I'd do well. In my last role, I was given an assignment to work on an internal start-up. I know it's not the same, but I think there were a lot of similarities that demonstrate I can thrive in an entrepreneurial environment. For example . . .

. . .

Concern: Honestly, it seems like a stretch that you'd want to leave your current job in California and move your family to the Midwest.

Response: Well, I can certainly understand that concern. I have never lived in the Midwest, and all my experience up to this point has been on the West Coast. However, we have been frustrated with the housing prices in California lately and really want to be in a more affordable place. We've made a few visits and have gotten our minds around the Midwest. In fact, we're really excited about it!

. . .

Concern: You may be overqualified for this job.

Response: Thanks for the compliment! I can understand how that would be a concern. You wouldn't want someone to get bored or leave. However, as I've studied this position and learned from you in this interview, I think there are a lot of growth opportunities for me here. I am looking at this as a long-term opportunity with the company because there are a lot of things that excite me about it. I'm confident that, while on paper I may be a little overqualified, I will be able to grow my responsibilities and find additional ways to contribute.

. . .

Concern: Your social media experience is mostly with Instagram. We really need someone who can help us get into TikTok.

Response: I can understand that concern. TikTok is trending right now, and you want to have that skill set. I've found, however, that a lot of skills I've learned are transferable. A lot of my Instagram work has focused on reels, which are the same video format as TikToks. And, while I haven't used TikTok in my latest job, I have used it personally, and I've studied how to leverage it and build audiences on a personal level, and I've grown my own personal following by 30 percent over the last two months. I'm confident that I could hit the ground running in building a TikTok audience for you.

• • •

Concern: This position requires three years of managing a team, and I'm just not sure if you have enough experience managing other people. Especially since a couple of the people reporting to you want this job!

Response: I can understand that for sure. Roles where people must come in and establish credibility with a team are extremely important, and it's a risk to bring someone in from the outside. And I do have only two years managing a team. However, during those two years I had tremendous success. My ratings as a boss were among the top in the company, and my team has a 100 percent retention rate. So, while I understand that I don't have the exact number of years listed on the description, I think the results I've shown while I was managing a team indicate that I can come in and do a fantastic job of leading this team.

Make Your Final Pitch

One surprising job interview insight came to me during a career boot camp I attended before starting business school. It was an intensive two-day course full of résumé writing, interview preparation, and expert presentations. One of the presenters was a seasoned human resources executive. He had worked for several large corporations and had hired and fired many people over more than three decades. During his presentation, he said, "One of the main reasons people don't get offers after interviewing is that the hiring managers don't think the interviewee would accept the offer. Hiring managers want to know that you are interested in the job. They want confidence that you'd accept the position if they offer it to you." It was a surprise to me because I didn't think companies thought that way or cared that much. Yet over the years, I've found that to be true. Not only do they want you to be a rock star, but they want to be reasonably sure that you'll take the job. If they don't feel that way, there is a decent chance they won't extend an offer. From that moment on, I've never finished a job interview without genuinely expressing my interest and enthusiasm for the position—and neither have my clients.

This doesn't have to be anything special. After you are done asking your questions, just tell them you love them again and tell them why. For example, "I just want to say thank you for interviewing me. This interview has helped me learn more about the company and the position, and I'm even more excited now than when I started the interview. I believe I'd be a great fit for your company, and I'm looking forward to the next steps." It's simple, but it works.

Reduce Stress with a Commitment

The aftermath of an interview can be one of the most stressful parts of the whole experience. It's a waiting game. The interview goes well, then a few days pass, then a week, then two weeks, then . . . anxiety. Sometimes it's because they aren't interested in you. Other times it's because the company is just slow and hasn't gotten the necessary approvals. I've even seen companies change their minds and close the position after the interview process.

All of this causes stress to build. Much of it is avoidable. When my clients ask me, "If I don't hear back from the company, how long should I wait before I follow up?" I always respond with a question: "Did they give you a time for when they'd get back to you?" Most of the time, the answer is no. But in the cases where they did provide a timeline, my answer is, "If their stated deadline to get back to you has passed, then it's okay to reach out."

If they don't volunteer a timeline to you in the interview, ask for one. A simple "What does your timeline look like to make a decision?" or "When should I expect to hear back from you?" will work. With a committed date, you'll have a lot less anxiety and a lot more power. No longer will you have to guess the right time to reach back out. When the date passes, it's perfectly logical to reach out to the hiring manager, kindly reference their previous commitment to you, and ask what's up. If they are vague about it and make excuses, tell them you understand, but get another commitment by asking them for a revised date. If they can't give you a date, propose a date you'll follow up with them and ask if that's okay. Be nice but keep them on the hook so you can ensure that your candidacy is progressing.

Chapter Summary

The end of the interview is your opportunity to finish strong.

If they ask you if you have any questions, avoid
- questions you ask only to look smart,

- questions that clearly put you and your career first,
- questions that require the interviewer to speculate,
- negative questions,
- questions that require long, complicated answers, and
- questions for which the interviewer likely doesn't know the answer.

Instead, ask engaging questions that

- genuinely interest you,
- are related to the job, and
- the interviewer is uniquely qualified to answer.

Never close the interview without resolving potential concerns.

Resolve them by using "I understand" and "however."

Make your final pitch by telling them you love them.

End with a committed timeline for when you can follow up.

Preparation Checklist Progress

Closing strong	
Have you prepared 2–3 engaging and positive questions?	✔
Are you ready to resolve concerns using "I understand" and "however"?	✔
Did you ask for a timeline of next steps?	✔
Did you tell them you love them one more time?	✔

eleven.
know your worth
Negotiating Your Best Offer

Sarah was willing to take a pay cut. She had spent five years working as a marketing manager for a large corporation, and after surviving several rounds of layoffs and organizational changes, she was burned out and miserable. She wanted out of her job so badly that she was willing to make a lot of concessions, including sacrificing her pay. It was at this point that she reached out to me for help.

After speaking with her for fifteen minutes, it was clear Sarah wasn't being rational. Her desire to get out of her current job was clouding her judgment to the point that she couldn't fully see reality. She didn't need to take a job with less pay. She had great experience, and the market was red hot for people with her skills. Not only was she in a great position to find another job, but she also had an opportunity to get a nice increase in compensation.

"Hold up, Sarah," I said. "Let's not worry about taking a pay cut just yet. Let's focus first on getting you some great interviews for jobs that have salaries in your range. Then let's make sure you nail the interviews so you can get an offer or two on the table. After that, let's talk money. I strongly doubt you'll have to take a pay cut."

She dutifully agreed to humor me and postpone the money discussion until an offer came in.

Within a month or so, she called to tell me she had received an offer and was excited about the position. We crafted a negotiation strategy, and a few days later, she signed an offer with a salary $20,000 more than her previous pay.

How did Sarah get a pay raise? Was it because she had great experience in a strong market? That certainly helped. But it was more than that. Sarah had learned not only her value in the marketplace but also how to realize that value. When it was time to fight for herself, she knew the negotiating points that mattered and those that didn't.

These salary negotiation principles are often hidden from plain view because money is a sensitive topic. Companies often keep salaries confidential because they don't want their competitors or other employees to find out what they pay people. Employees keep their salaries to themselves because it feels weird to tell other people what they make. I'm always amazed at how comfortable people are talking about sex, health care, their kids, and other matters that used to be relatively private. But money? It's still a personal matter for most people. Most people in my generation grew up having no clue how much money their parents made. As an adult, I have no idea what my adult siblings make. I can only guess what my closest friends make, but I don't know an exact number.

I'm not knocking this. Maybe kids don't show enough maturity and interest for parents to trust them. Maybe my siblings and I feel it would get too awkward if we shared how much money we all make. I'm not arguing for or against how to communicate about money in your close circles. I'm merely illustrating the secrecy about money. People don't just keep their personal financial information from strangers. They keep it from their own flesh and blood.

It's no wonder, then, that salary negotiations can be so stressful. Not only are many candidates raised to believe money shouldn't be openly discussed, but then they face a salary negotiation process that is deliberately opaque.

Well, this all ends now. In this chapter, I'll discuss the ins and outs of compensation negotiations. Once we're done, there should be no doubt in your mind about how to approach negotiating your offer to reach the best possible outcome.

Think Milk

Allow me a crude, if not offensive, analogy. You, as a job candidate, are like a jug of milk. That's right, milk—or any other commodity for that matter. Like commodities, employees are purchased in an open marketplace that is based on supply and demand. When demand for employees exceeds supply, employees have the upper hand and salaries rise, along with job security. When supply exceeds demand, corporations have the upper hand, making salaries stagnate and creating the potential for layoffs.

You may not like thinking about yourself as a commodity, but it can be useful when negotiating an offer. As you prepare to make the case for why you should get what you want, ask yourself, "How does a commodity get a raise?" Then ask yourself, "How does a commodity not get a raise?" Knowing the answers to these questions can help you focus your discussion on the things that actually matter to the marketplace and avoid focusing on things that will get you nowhere.

Stick with me a little longer on my milk analogy. If a jug of milk wanted to get a salary increase by raising its shelf price, it would have to justify the price increase to the market. Some of the justifications would work, and others wouldn't. Here are a few reasons milk might give that the market wouldn't care about.

Fairness: A jug of milk at my local grocery store can complain all it wants about the fact that it's priced at $3.50. Perhaps it thinks it should command a price of $3.99 and feels that it is not being treated fairly because it's a hard-working gallon of milk and it's just not fair that the juice and soda get all the glory by being more expensive. While I may sympathize with it, I still won't be willing to pay more for it than the market price tag on the shelf. If it's priced too high, I'll go get another jug of the exact same quality milk somewhere else. Why? Because I don't care about the jug's perception of fairness. I care that I am getting a fair price for what I'm buying.

Similarly, arguing as a job candidate that you should get a higher salary based on "fairness" won't get you very far because it's an argument that's all about you and your perceptions, not about what you are providing to the employer.

Competence: Proficiency is expected from commodities. Milk should look like milk, smell like milk, and taste like milk. It should do its job. If it doesn't, it gets thrown away. Thus, as a candidate, making the point that you are qualified for the job is not a strong argument that you should get anything more than average pay.

Need: You may need more money because you want to improve your situation, feed your family, or purchase a car, but those factors don't have anything to do with the value you are providing in the marketplace. I've never heard of a successful salary discussion where the employee's key argument was "because I need the money."

Each of these justifications—fairness, competence, and need—are focused inward. They address only what the employee wants. But to get the employer to care about your salary requirements, you need to focus the conversation outward and talk about the value you bring.

Several years ago, a friend of mine secured an offer to be the CEO of a large food cooperative. As he was negotiating his salary with the company's board of directors, one of them said to him, "You know, the salary you are asking for is more than the governor of our state." My friend responded, "That's because I'm going to do a lot more for you than the governor will!" His statement illustrates the point perfectly.

Back to milk (sorry). Here are a few justifications for a pay raise milk could give that the market would care about.

Points of difference: Plain nonfat milk is plain nonfat milk. There isn't anything special about it, so its price likely isn't anything special, either. But organic milk, or milk fortified with extra protein, or milk that has added vitamins for kids? Now, that's a different discussion. These little extras create additional value for consumers and therefore have the potential to command a higher price.

As an employee, think about what you have done above and beyond what is listed in your job description. Do you have more experience than is required in the job description? Do you have a unique type of experience that other candidates don't have? Are you the "go-to" expert for certain types of work? You don't have to meet every single qualification, but if you can figure out one or two things that make you different, especially things relevant to the job description, they will almost certainly listen to you.

High switching costs: When I'm at the grocery store and my kids are whining, I am in no mood to bargain shop. I want my jug of milk to be priced fairly, of course, but I'm not going to drive to another store just to get a twenty-cent discount. Similarly, when companies spend a lot of time and energy finding the right person and making an offer to that person, they don't want to start all over. This gives you a little negotiating leverage. We'll talk about this more later in the chapter.

Market dynamics: In the end, a jug of milk is worth what someone is willing to pay for it. If you have done your research and discovered that the market commands a higher price for the experiences and skills that you have, you have a solid negotiating point.

So all of us are commodities operating within a system. That system may seem demoralizing and unfair to some, but that's because they don't understand the rules by which it operates. Albert Einstein said, "You have to learn the rules of the game. And then you have to play better than anyone else." You now understand the rules of the game—focus outward instead of inward. Now let's learn the details of how to play.

The Ten Laws of Compensation Negotiations

Many people believe that compensation negotiations are so contextual and unique to each circumstance that you can't possibly give broad advice on the topic. This is understandable. Context matters. But I've also found that there are ten laws of compensation negotiations that are wise to follow, no matter what the circumstance. They've proven to be true again and again in my coaching practice and in my career. If I think back to all the times a client of mine has gotten compensation negotiations wrong, it's been because they violated one of these ten laws. Here they are:

First: the best time to negotiate your compensation is when you have an offer in writing.

You have the most negotiating leverage when you have a written offer in hand because that's when you know for sure that they want to hire you. Before that, all conversations about money are hypothetical and can't be trusted. In fact, it's often unfair for a potential employer to ask a candidate about salary during the interview process. It makes the candidate feel like they need to aim low so that they won't be disqualified for the job. That's why it's often best to punt and tell them that you first want to make sure that you are a great fit with the organization through the interview process and that you are confident you can come to a compensation agreement that works for both parties.

Of course, there are circumstances when it's okay to discuss compensation before you receive an official offer. For example, if you have a lot of other options and don't want to waste your time unless you know the compensation meets your requirements, it makes sense to have the conversation up front. Other times, someone may call you to extend a verbal offer and let you know that a written offer is coming. This is a great sign, but it is not an offer. But if you feel like it's been a clean process up to that point and you have reasonable confidence that a written offer is coming, it's usually okay to negotiate a little at that point. But even then, you shouldn't negotiate the offer fully. Only when you see all the details in writing can you properly evaluate and respond.

Second: any agreements, promises, or statements not in writing should not be taken seriously.

Several years ago, I had a great offer from a company. I wanted to take it, but I wasn't completely satisfied with the salary. I went back and forth with the hiring manager a bit. We got it raised a little, but not as much as I thought it should be. I told this to the hiring manager, and he told me about the upward mobility at the company and said that within a year I should be able to get a promotion and a raise. That ultimately convinced me, and I accepted the offer.

Big mistake. Not my accepting the offer—that was still a good choice. The mistake was thinking our conversation about promotion represented even a faint commitment. Once I got to the company, I was assigned to work for someone else, and the original hiring manager no longer had a say in my career progression. I eventually did get promoted but not because of that conversation. This might seem obvious to you. You may think I should have known better. You're right. But when you are emotionally tied to a position and really want to accept an offer, it's easy to believe what you want to believe.

This problem of perceived broken promises happens all the time. I've had people working for me tell me that I should give them a raise because a previous manager made verbal commitments to them. While I sympathized with them, I had to remind them that they would get promoted based either on readiness or on company commitments in writing.

It's not necessarily bad that people make verbal commitments in the recruiting process. It's a sign that they like you and want you to work there. Just recognize that if you really want that commitment to come true, you need to get it in writing. If it's not in writing, you should make your decision with the assumption that verbal commitments of pay increases or promotions are not firm.

Third: it's best to be paid what you are worth, not a lot more or a lot less.

There is a prevailing belief in hiring that the aim of the employee should be to get the highest possible salary and that the aim of the employer should be to pay the lowest possible salary. This will not set either the employee or employer up for a successful relationship. Either the employee will be upset in a year after finding out that they were lowballed—and trust me, they will find out eventually—or the employer will be upset that they are paying too much for an employee and look to either make a downward pay adjustment or let the employee go.

That's why both employer and employee should aim for a compensation package that matches the value the employee provides. It sets the relationship up for long-term success because both the employer and employee will feel like they are getting a fair deal. It will also provide room for long-term career progression.

Fourth: compensation is about salary and so much more

There are several points of a job offer up for negotiation. Salary is an important—perhaps the most important—part of the offer.

It sets the baseline for future pay increases and is the starting point for negotiations should you ever leave for another job. But there is so much more to discuss beyond salary. Below is a list. Not every job has each of these things, but these are all things that I've seen up for negotiation.

- *Annual bonus:* many roles have a bonus target, which is typically a percentage of your salary.
- *Signing bonus:* to get you to join, some companies are willing to throw in a little cash. This is easy for them to do because it's a "one-time" payment and doesn't mess with their structured compensation.
- *Time off:* you can negotiate on weeks of vacation, especially if you are coming from an organization where you have more of it.
- *Remote work:* some companies are willing to let you work from home once in a while, even if it's an in-office job.
- *Bonus or equity "make goods":* in executive roles, companies will often pay you a portion of the equity or bonus money you are walking away from to secure you.

There are many other things, such as tuition reimbursement, travel expenses, severance packages, car allowances, gym memberships, phone allowances, and more. The list seems to keep growing as companies fight for talent. Some of these things are nonnegotiable, others are highly negotiable. It depends on the company. At my level, I like to focus on salary, bonus, and equity. Once that is done, there may be a couple of other things I care about, but not much.

Fifth: companies are much more willing to negotiate if they believe you will accept the offer.

When a potential employer knows that a candidate wants to take the job, they are much more likely to negotiate. So you should let them know how excited you are about the position and hint that you want to take the position, pending negotiations going well. This process of showing enthusiasm for the position starts in the interview, of course, but it can be reinforced in the negotiation process to help get things to the finish line.

Sixth: don't underestimate the power of likability.

Compensation negotiations can be hard. It can be unpleasant and even frightening to negotiate your compensation because there is so much at stake. But just because negotiations can get challenging doesn't mean they have to be adversarial. Things will go better if you approach negotiations with optimism and a positive intent, based on the belief that both parties are trying to strike a deal that you can both live with.

Seventh: you likely won't burn bridges by negotiating hard.

Companies understand that great candidates want to negotiate. Strong negotiations almost never result in a rescinded offer or in an employee entering the company with a bad reputation. Negotiate hard, hold your ground, and, when you start at the company, it will likely all be forgotten.

There are examples, however, in which negotiations do affect a person's reputation. Sometimes employees want to negotiate back and forth four or five times. It's best to be buttoned up on exactly what you want and what you can live with up front, so negotiations don't extend beyond a couple of rounds.

Eighth: knowledge is power.

If the salary range is not posted, you should use the skills laid out in chapter 2 on getting inside information to find out the pay range for this role. Research online; talk to trusted friends. Don't go in blind. A company may deliberately keep it private to hold more leverage, but that shouldn't stop you from getting the information.

Ninth: a rushed deal is usually a bad deal for one party.

Sometimes things move fast, and it just works out serendipitously that both parties live happily ever after. But most of the time, if the process is rushed or the company imposes a fast deadline, something is missed, and one party is upset later to find out that they aren't getting exactly what they thought they were getting. Usually, it's the candidate that winds up realizing they should have asked for more money or more vacation or more of something else.

If you aren't feeling comfortable with the offer but are out of time, ask for more time. Tell them you are thrilled about the offer, but you just need a little bit of time to fully understand all the elements of the offer because you want to be "all in" when you accept it. If you have a written offer, the company will almost always accommodate this. With a little more time, you'll either be able to get comfortable with the offer, or you'll want to further negotiate the points that need work. You may not get any further than you would have had you quickly accepted the offer, but at least you will have the satisfaction of knowing you did everything you could to fight for yourself.

Tenth: your current salary can be a good negotiating point, or it can be a liability.

Many times in my negotiations, I've flat-out told an employer my salary and then told them exactly what it would take to get me to switch jobs. This put me in a good position because I already came to the table with a strong salary and employers understand that getting a person to leave a job to take another usually requires an increase in compensation.

But if you are going for a major pay bump or coming right out of school, you likely don't have this luxury. In this case, you'll need to build your case based on the salary range for the position and on your ability to do the job well. Sometimes an employer will ask you, point-blank, what your current salary is. You don't have to tell them but, if you don't, they will think you are trying to hide something. It's usually best to respond honestly and make the case for why you should get paid more.

The Four Steps in Every Salary Negotiation

To negotiate your salary well, you'll follow these four steps:

Step one: identify exactly what you want. You probably have one to two rounds of negotiation before the process starts to feel petty and annoying for both parties, so there is not much use in wasting time going back and forth without knowing what you want. Know exactly which negotiating points are most important to you and start there. Don't try to take them all at once. Pick the top two or three and go for it.

Step two: prepare your justification. Your hiring manager probably doesn't have the power to give you what you want; they likely need to get approval from other people in the organization. To get approval, they'll need reasons why they should give you what you want. As you develop your reasons, remember what we covered early in the chapter: fairness, competence, and need don't matter. Market dynamics and points of difference do matter.

Step three: rehearse your response. This is a high-stakes, potentially emotional situation. You want to deliver your response confidently and without flinching. It's worth practicing a few times to make sure you have your talking points down. If you are negotiating over the phone, even better because you can have notes in hand.

Step four: deliver. I prefer to deliver my talking points through a direct conversation, either virtually or in person. I've found that it's so much better than email because I can fully portray my enthusiasm for the position and deliver my talking points in a personal way that is unlikely to be misunderstood. After delivering my talking points through a conversation, I follow up in writing, so my reasons are well documented, and the hiring manager can refer to them when arguing my case. I recommend this in-person or over-the-phone method to my clients. It portrays strength and confidence. Cutting straight to an email fails to make a personal connection and leaves too much open to interpretation.

Examples

Let's look at some examples of what a great delivery sounds like.

Example one: Mark has just secured a written offer from a major airline for a position as a financial analyst. The offer includes a salary of $65,000 per year with a $10,000 signing bonus attached to it. It also includes two weeks of vacation and a full health-care and retirement package. From Mark's research, he knows that the health-care and retirement package is standard across the company, so he knows there is no wiggle room. He's decided to focus on salary, signing bonus, and vacation. He calls the hiring manager, Terence, and says:

> *Hi, Terence! First, let me say I am thrilled with this opportunity and the offer that I received. I am really excited about this position and want to make this work. I'd like to ask for a few things to make sure this offer works on my end.*
>
> *First, I'd like to ask that the salary be raised by $5,000 to $70,000 and that my signing bonus be raised by $5,000 to $15,000. There are several reasons I'm asking for this compensation adjustment. First, I bring five years of financial analytical skills to the table versus the three years stated in the job description. Second, during those five years, I've demonstrated my ability to get results based on my rapid promotions and contributions to the business that we discussed in my interview. Third, based on my assessment, the signing bonus will help me move to this location and get fully settled and do more for you. Fourth, my current salary is close to this, and I believe I will be getting a raise if I stay where I am. And*

*finally, based on my research, the amount and type of experi-
ence merits this adjustment in my opinion.*

*The last thing I'd like to ask for pertains to vacation. I have
three weeks of vacation at my current position, so I'm asking that
you match that.*

*I'm happy to put this all in an email for you. Again, I'm really
excited about this opportunity. How does all of this sound to
you?*

Example two: Lisa has secured a written offer for a marketing
manager position from an online women's apparel company. The
salary is $120,000 per year, plus an annual performance bonus
of 10 percent of her salary, or $12,000 per year. The job requires
her to move from Detroit to Seattle, so a full moving package
is attached to the offer, which includes moving all her belong-
ings, covering closing costs on the sale of her home and the
purchase of her new one, and a stipend of $10,000 to cover
flights, hotel stays, and other incidentals. The offer also includes
a full health and 401(k) package. She is currently walking away
from a $105,000 salary and a 10 percent bonus. She also has
some stock in her old company that vests in one year. It's worth
$20,000. She wants to focus her negotiation first on maximiz-
ing her salary and bonus and then on making up the equity
from which she is walking away. She calls Kara, the hiring manager, and says:

*Kara, I'm thrilled about this offer. I feel like this position is such a
great fit for me, based on my skill set and the things I'm trying to
accomplish in my career. I think the offer is looking good, but I'd*

like to ask that the salary and bonus be adjusted. I'd like the salary to be bumped to $130,000 per year and my bonus target to be bumped to 15 percent. I'm asking this based on my assessment of similar manager-level jobs like this. I am happy to email you some of those facts. Also, this is a big move for me and my family, and to make a move like this to a more expensive market like Seattle, I would expect at least a $20,000 pay increase to what I'm already making, plus the potential for more upside on the bonus side, especially considering the $20,000 of equity I'd be walking away from in accepting this offer.

Let's suppose Kara comes back with a salary of $130,000 but is not able to budget for the bonus target. Lisa could then respond with the following:

Thank you for working on the salary and I understand about the bonus target. The biggest struggle for me is the equity I'm leaving behind. If you aren't able to build that into the bonus, would you be able to issue me an additional $15,000 as a one-time signing bonus to cover this? This would help me feel like I'm being made whole and would make me thrilled to accept this offer!

Chapter Summary

When it comes to salary negotiations, focus outward instead of inward. Fairness, competence, and need don't matter. Points of difference, high switching costs, and market dynamics do matter.

The ten laws of compensations negotiations are:

1. The best time to negotiate your compensation is when you have an offer in writing.

2. Any agreements, promises, or statements not in writing should not be taken seriously.

3. It's best to be paid what you are worth, not a lot more or a lot less.

4. Compensation is about salary and so much more.

5. Companies are much more willing to negotiate if they believe you will accept the offer.

6. Don't underestimate the power of likability.

7. You likely won't burn bridges by negotiating hard.

8. Knowledge is power.

9. A rushed deal is usually a bad deal for one party or the other.

10. Your current salary can be a good negotiating point, or it can be a liability.

The four steps in salary negotiations are:

1. Identify what you want and what you can live with.

2. Prepare your justification.

3. Rehearse your response.

4. Deliver your response through a live conversation.

conclusion.

Learn, Build, and Contribute in Your New Job

I f this book has done its job, you will soon be starting a new position after having interviewed well and negotiated a great offer. Congratulations! You now have a new challenge: thriving in your new position. Thriving means starting your new role with momentum. It means enjoying what you are doing and the people with whom you are doing it, feeling that you are doing great, meaningful work. Most important, it means feeling that your future is bright at your new company.

Many employees don't feel this way. In fact, many don't even make it to their one-year anniversaries. One study conducted by the Work Institute reported that, in 2020, 40 percent of participants who reported quitting their jobs said they quit in their first year of employment. Clearly, many employees aren't thriving in their new roles.

But you can and you will! When I help clients land new jobs, they usually ask me the following question after they've signed an offer: "Sam, how do I do well in my new position?" The answer to that question usually leads to more coaching work where I help them succeed in the first critical months of employment. As a result of this coaching, I've had a front-row seat to a lot of new employee experiences. I've seen what works and what doesn't. I've witnessed employees who thrive and those who flounder. And, to close this book, I will tell you how to do it. (After all, I'd like you to read this book again, but not in six months.) There are some important things you must do to start your new job off strong. Do them well, and I promise you will be in a position of momentum and strength within the first three months at your company.

Manage Your Manager

Your relationship with your boss is the most important relationship you have at your new job. It's more important than your relationship with peers, direct reports, and people in other departments. If your relationship with your boss is weak, your job will be draining, stressful, and downright miserable enough to make you consider leaving. But if it is strong, you will be on the path to winning at your company, resulting in more responsibility, more advancement, and more money in your pocket.

You must build a strong relationship of trust with your manager immediately. You may get a great manager who takes the lead in building a relationship with you or you may get one who doesn't seem to care. But this shouldn't matter to you. For you, having a great relationship with your boss is not a game of chance but rather something you take charge of from day one on the job.

One way to build trust with your manager is to create an action plan for yourself and present it to her a few days after joining the organization. This plan could be for a specific project you've been given or for your whole job. It should include your interpretation of your responsibilities, a game plan showing how you are going to fulfill them, and a timeline of milestones. Doing this for your boss will not only show initiative but will also give her the opportunity to provide you with feedback. This will save you hours of time because you'll know which parts of your plan your boss cares about the most.

A second way to build trust is to overcommunicate with her, especially in the beginning. Bosses get anxious when they don't feel up to speed on what their employees are working on. If your boss doesn't know what you are working on, she can't update her boss on your progress and certainly can't certify that you are off to a great start. So you should give your boss frequent updates, via email, text, or in-person conversations, with details on what you are working on and how your projects are progressing. You won't know in the beginning how much your boss wants updates from you, but over time you'll get into a good rhythm. Push yourself to communicate more than you think you need to. It's better in the beginning for your boss to tell you to pull back a little than to tell you that you aren't communicating enough.

Build a Relationship With Everyone You Will Work With

Being new at the company gives you a perfect excuse to set up thirty-minute meetings with those you will be working with, including peers, superiors, potential mentors, and people in other departments. This is your free chance to establish personal connections. You don't want your first interaction with someone from another department to be when you need something from them. Rather, you want to have already taken them to lunch, to know about their kids and where they went to college, and to understand how you can both help one another succeed. So ask your boss for a list of people you should meet and set up times when you can get to know them. Ask for advice. After the meeting, ask them, "Who else should I get to know?"

Another way to build personal relationships is to find ways to help people out before they help you. Jump in and make yourself useful. Say yes to things. All of this will pay off soon down the road.

Listen More Than You Speak

Too many new employees think that the way to succeed in a new position is to shake things up, to establish themselves by making a lot of changes. As a result, they make critical errors because they fail to properly assess the culture and background at the organization. And worse, they come off as arrogant, which is way worse than if you had just shut up in the first place.

Remember, most problems sound easy to solve when you first hear about them. It's only when you dig in and truly listen that you discover how complex they really are. So listen and learn from others. Validate people when they explain things to you. When offering opinions, recognize that you could be wrong. You don't have to solve everything all at once. Play the long game and build trust through listening. You'll have plenty of time to solve problems as you become more familiar with the job.

Nail Your First Assignments

Listening and learning doesn't mean you can't find ways to contribute meaningfully. Whatever your first assignments are, no matter how trivial, do them with excellence. These assignments set the tone for your employment and will lead to bigger, more important assignments.

Make Your Own Good Luck

I've been at this career thing for nearly two decades. I've worked for organizations both big and small. I've observed and coached people at all levels and have watched careers come and go. One question I've thought about all these years is, "What role does luck play in career success?" I'm convinced that luck plays a significant role, but that its power diminishes over time. That is, short-term career results are nearly impossible to predict because they can be based on things completely out of your control. Companies make crazy decisions. Economic cycles play out. Layoffs happen. Bosses can suck.

But long-term career results are relatively easy to predict. Things tend to work out for those who keep trying. Like the stock price of strong companies, short-term career bumps smooth out over time, becoming part of a story of a steady, upward pattern of growth. Great employees can be denied a promotion only so many times before they get it. A great candidate can only be rejected so many times before landing a great job. Eventually, hard work, practice, and relentlessness win.

Likewise, the principles in this book don't guarantee you an offer from your next job interview. There are too many factors outside of your control to count on that. Perhaps the interview is merely a formality and they've already picked an internal candidate. Maybe they will close the position and hire no one after interviewing. Or maybe another candidate knows the CEO of the company. Sometimes, there's nothing you can do about short-term setbacks. But if you keep applying the principles in this book, interview after interview, you will eventually land a great job. More importantly, you'll build the muscle that will allow you to land great jobs again and again. Then you'll look back and realize that, while you may have had a couple of nice breaks in your career, you largely made your own good luck.

And that's what I wish for you. Nothing but your own good luck.

index.

about the author.

SAM OWENS is the founder of Sam's Career Talk, where he provides career coaching services and helps people land their dream jobs and thrive in them. He is also a chief marketing officer who has worked for three multibillion-dollar companies in the consumer packaged goods (CPG) industry. Currently, Sam is chief marketing officer at Freezing Point, the makers of Frazil slushies. He and his wife, Gina, have four children and live in Erie, Colorado.